DATE DUE

APR 2 9 1996	

GAYLORD   PRINTED IN U.S.A.

Fundamentals of Petroleum Trading

Fundamentals of Petroleum Trading

Hossein Razavi
and
Fereidun Fesharaki

New York
Westport, Connecticut
London

Library of Congress Cataloging-in-Publication Data

Razavi, Hossein.
  Fundamentals of petroleum trading / Hossein Razavi and Fereidun
Fesharaki.
    p. cm.
  Includes bibliographical references and index.
  ISBN 0-275-93920-0 (alk. paper)
  1. Petroleum industry and trade. 2. Commodity exchanges.
I. Fesharaki, Fereidun. II. Title.
HG6047.P47R39   1991
332.63'28—dc20   91-8072

British Library Cataloguing in Publication Data is available.

Library of Congress Catalog Card Number: 91-8072
ISBN: 0-275-93920-0

First published in 1991

Praeger Publishers, One Madison Avenue, New York, NY 10010
An imprint of Greenwood Publishing Group, Inc.

Printed in the United States of America

∞™

The paper used in this book complies with the Permanent
Paper Standard issued by the National Information Standards
Organization (Z39.48—1984).

10 9 8 7 6 5 4 3 2 1

To Pouneh

Contents

CONTENTS

Preface

Until as recently as the early 1970s, the main channel for oil supply was the integrated system of the major oil companies. Each company had its own source of crude oil supply as well as the capacity to refine it. Petroleum products outside this closed system, either released from it due to imbalances between refinery output and market demand, or refined independently of it, constituted the basis for spot trading. The volume of spot trading was limited to around 5 percent of the total oil trade, while the remaining 95 percent was based on contracts specifying prices and quantities over relatively long periods of time. Even that limited amount of spot trading was conducted in a very simple manner. Most of the trade was in the form of uninvoiced exchanges and based on personal trust, characterizing an era that many oil company executives remember as the "good old days."

Today, spot and spot-related trades comprise some 80 percent to 85 percent of internationally traded petroleum. Petroleum trading has not only developed into one of the largest worldwide commodity markets but has turned into an increasingly complex business. A spot trade involves millions of dollars and is carried out by sale and purchase agreements containing numerous safeguard measures. A cargo of oil may be bought and sold more than thirty times before reaching its final destination. Still, each seller or buyer may utilize "petroleum futures," "options on futures," and other financial instruments to hedge against the risk of possible price fluctuations. The interlinkages among spot trading, futures markets, and contract sales have changed the nature of the petroleum business from its traditional straightforward production-oriented approach to a complex portfolio management environment.

Within this new environment, all parties involved in the production, distribution, and consumption of petroleum need to acquire a fundamental understanding of the workings and the issues involved in the new era of petroleum trading. This book is intended to provide such understanding. It provides a detailed description of petroleum spot markets, futures and options trading, and their interlinkages with contract sales.

Chapter 1 gives an overview of recent developments in spot, futures, and contract trading. Chapters 2 to 4 provide an analysis of spot and spot-related deals. Chapters 5 to 8 describe the mechanics, organization, and evolution of petroleum futures markets and options trading. Finally, chapters 9 to 12 discuss the interactions among various segments of the market, including spot and futures trading, petroleum stock building, and the Organization of Petroleum-Exporting Countries (OPEC).

PART ONE

The Setting

CHAPTER 1

An Overview of Present Trading Practices

Crude oil and petroleum products are traded in either of two categories: by contract (sometimes referred to as term sales) or by spot transactions. A contract sale, as the term indicates, commits the buyer and seller to trade oil over a set period of time and often at fixed prices. In the past, this period could have been as far ahead as three years. More recently, both the contract period and the price have been much more flexible. Spot sales, on the other hand, refer to short-term trading, usually involving one cargo of oil per deal, with each deal struck at an agreed price for prompt lifting or delivery. Spot trading can thus be defined as a process by which cargoes of petroleum are exchanged on a day-to-day basis rather than under long-term contracts.

During the last decade, spot trading in petroleum has grown dramatically, from 10–15 percent to about 30–35 percent of total volume traded in the international market. In addition, a new wave of spot-related transactions that link the contract price to spot market price has emerged. These deals, which were virtually nonexistent before the 1980s, now comprise an estimated 50–55 percent of total trade.

This chapter briefly reviews recent developments in the spot market and the interactions of this market with contract sales and futures trading.

THE UNDERLYING FORCES BEHIND DEVELOPMENT OF SPOT MARKETS

Since the age of barter economies, the starting point of trade for all grains and minerals has been the spot market. In this sense, a spot market is the "natural" market and the contract market is a special arrangement introduced at a later stage to cope with certain problems. The main problem with spot trading is that neither the producer nor the consumer can predict the price and quantity and thus are unable to plan their business. The extent of this problem is, of course, different for various commodities depending on the volatility of the market and the lead time needed for investment decisions. The most difficult trading situation, and the one typical of the oil industry, is that in which: (a) the supply of the commodity, and thereby its price, is subject to manipulation; and (b) there is a long investment lead time for both producers and consumers, who may, in turn, use this commodity to produce other goods. Faced with the unpredictability of spot trading and the problems it poses for planning, both producers and consumers search for contractual arrangements that provide predictability in price and quantity over a specified period of time. Thus, the development of a contract market is mainly a response to the need for planning of business activities on the part of both the producer and the consumer.

While contracts facilitate the planning and management of businesses, they take away flexibility. Term contracts are normally made for long periods of time and at predetermined prices. When business conditions are relatively stable, the rigidity of these contracts is acceptable. But when markets become unstable, rigid contracts can hinder efficient business operations. The attempt to balance the benefits and drawbacks of both systems has resulted in two approaches to trading. In the short and medium terms, producers and consumers need flexible arrangements—that is, they need to be able to combine spot and contract trading in their portfolios in order to keep some flexibility (through spot trading) while preserving predictability (through contract trading). The composition of such a portfolio will vary among business entities and over time. As a result, the industry's trade, at the macro level, will undergo periodic shifts between spot and contract trading. In the long run, the industry will embark on a search for "more flexible contracts." This would include contracts with flexible pricing and delivery arrangements as well as contracts that can be sold to a third party. There is, of course, a limit to this flexibility. If contracts were to become too flexible, they would no longer be contracts.

The search for flexible contracts will eventually lead to the introduction of futures markets. These markets will, indirectly, provide contract trading with price flexibility and transferability options while allowing contracts to be based on long-term delivery and fixed-price conditions. (See chapter 6 for a discussion of the interaction between the contract and futures markets.)

After futures markets are incorporated into overall trading practices, both buyers and sellers are better off if they return to long-term contract trading, because this type of trading can be combined with futures market activity to keep the flexibility needed to cope with the changing business environment. The extent of the return to long-term contract trading would depend on the extent to which futures markets have developed. If they are worldwide and cover a sufficiently long period of time into the future, then there is little incentive for spot trading. Under such circumstances, most sellers and buyers find it advantageous to use contract trading; the spot market's role will then diminish to a residual or balancing market. In practice, however, there are limitations to the development of futures markets in terms of geographical coverage, lead time, and product coverage, and thus the return to contract trading will remain far less than perfect.

VARIOUS STAGES OF DEVELOPMENT OF PETROLEUM SPOT MARKETS

Spot transactions in oil have existed as long as the industry itself. Today, however, the spot market normally refers to spot trading in Rotterdam, New York Harbor, and a few other centers. These markets have become established only in the past two decades. They have developed in four distinct stages, which are explained below.

Stage 1: The Spot Market Functioning as the Residual Market

Almost all oil companies face the problem of matching their refinery output with the market's current demand for various products. They have deficits of some products and surpluses of others. The company may balance these deficits and surpluses through the use of storage and/ or shipment facilities. But quite often it is more economical to balance them by swapping or selling and buying some products on the spot market. This was primarily the function that the spot market served in its early stages of development in the 1950s and 1960s.

The role of the spot market at this stage can be described as a residual channel of oil trade. The main channel for oil supply was the integrated system of the major oil companies: each company had its own supply of crude oil as well as the capacity to refine it. Petroleum products outside this closed system, either released from it due to imbalances between refinery output and market demand, or refined independently of it, constituted the basis for spot trading. The volume of spot trading was limited to around 5 percent of total trade, while the remaining 95 percent was based on contracts specifying prices and quantities over relatively long periods.

Stage 2: Shift from a Residual to a Marginal Market

After the 1973–74 oil crisis, the spot market began to play a marginal role in petroleum trading, that is, small but significant trading as opposed to the small and insignificant trading of the residual market. The significance is, of course, in terms of the impact on the main (contract) market. When the spot market serves a residual role it basically follows contract prices (usually with a discount or a premium) without significantly affecting these prices. But when the spot market serves a marginal role, it becomes an indicator of overall market conditions. As in any other business, when decisions are made in the petroleum industry, they are determined by marginal results. The cost and revenue of producing or processing the marginal barrel constitute the basis of decision-making in many planning areas—especially in refinery operations.

The spot market's shift from a residual to a marginal market occurred in 1975–78, when low spot prices were used as indicators of soft market conditions by both the petroleum industry and the governments of consuming countries (to set price control policies). The shift accelerated after 1979 when it was demonstrated that the spot market could play this role under both tight and soft market conditions.

Stage 3: Turning into a Major Market

Despite the significance of spot transactions to the industry's planning and pricing policies, their volume remained small during the second stage of market development. It was only after 1983 that spot and spot-related trade began to grow appreciably. Between 1983 and 1985, spot and spot-related transactions grew to account for 80–90 percent of internationally traded oil. Several factors contributed to this rapid growth. First, excess capacity in the refining industry forced refiners to fight for their survival. Refiners were forced to use the most economical way of procuring crude oil. They increased their refinery throughput to the point where the price of a marginal barrel of product covered the marginal operating cost. This brought about a shift from term-contract arrangements to spot purchasing of crude to take advantage of flexible (declining) spot prices over rigid contract prices. "Refining for the spot market" also became a common practice. That is, despite a tradition of refiners' determining their level of operation in the light of market demand and selling only surpluses on the spot market, excess capacity forced many refiners to refine and sell on the spot markets as long as they could cover operating costs.

Second, as the member countries of the Organization of Petroleum-Exporting Countries (OPEC) began to lose their market share, they began to engage in so-called spot-related sales to recapture lost sales. These spot-related sales included variable price contracts, barter trade, netback pricing deals, etc.

Stage 4: Parallel Function with Futures Markets

Markets in petroleum futures developed in response to instability of spot prices. The first generation of petroleum futures, including a crude oil contract on the New York Cotton Exchange and a Bunker C and gasoil contract on the New York Mercantile Exchange (NYMEX), was introduced in 1974.

None of the first-generation contracts attracted the petroleum industry, and all faded into obscurity. The most important reason for this failure was that petroleum prices did not fluctuate as expected. The international spot price of crude oil stayed between \$10.30 and \$10.40 per barrel (b) during the period from October 1974 to December 1975. Price stability was further reinforced in the United States by the Energy Policy and Conservation Act (1975), which, by limiting the annual increase in the crude oil price, led to reasonable predictability in petroleum prices.

The second generation of petroleum futures began with the introduction of a heating oil and heavy fuel contract on NYMEX in November 1978. The heating oil contract was a success because:

- Fuel oil had been exempted from price controls in more than forty U.S. states in 1976;
- The international price of oil became very volatile after 1978; and
- The complete deregulation of the U.S. oil price by the Reagan administration in February 1981 forged a stronger link between U.S. prices and volatile international prices.

The success of the heating oil contract encouraged NYMEX and other exchanges (Chicago Board of Trade, Chicago Mercantile Exchange, and International Petroleum Exchange of London) to introduce other petroleum futures. Among them, the crude oil contract introduced on NYMEX in March 1983 was the most significant: it expanded the potential for trading petroleum futures and substantially intensified the interaction between the futures and spot markets. Indeed, it was after the introduction of this contract that the petroleum industry began to take futures trading seriously. The significance of this contract was in:

- Its "cash market," that is, the crude oil spot market, being one of the largest commodity markets in the world;
- The complementary role of this contract in providing the industry's requirement of a crude/product mix of contracts before effectively utilizing petroleum futures for hedging purposes; and
- The fact that it soon developed into a price signaling channel for crude oil traders, especially in the United States.

At Stage 4, petroleum spot markets and futures trading are both still growing and increasing their roles in the industry's decision-making process. At the same time, the two markets interact, compete, and complement each other. As has been the case in the development of other commodity markets, the coexistence of spot and futures trading is a sign of a maturing market.

INTERACTIONS WITH CONTRACT MARKETS

In general, interactions between contract markets and spot trading are numerous, complicated, and difficult to trace. However, in the case of petroleum, the traditional structure of the market and, in particular, the different behaviors of the independent companies and the major oil companies facilitate the analysis of these interactions. Although it may no longer be the case, for almost two decades the pricing policy of the major oil companies was associated with contract markets, whereas the independent companies followed spot market directives. Beginning in the early 1970s, contracts were signed between the major oil companies and the governments of oil-producing countries, which had taken over the production of crude oil. The companies would then refine the crude in their own refineries or resell it to third-party customers, including some independents and government-owned companies in consuming countries. Thus, the major companies were the main channel of contract trading in the petroleum market. The independent companies, on the other hand, bought some of their requirements from the large companies but relied heavily on the spot market.

The flexibility of the independents in adjusting between sources of supply provided them with an opportunity to gain from spot trading under soft market conditions. They utilized this opportunity very effectively. For example, during the slack period 1975–78, independents were able to buy cheap crude and products on the spot market and undersell the retail outlets of the major companies (the majors) in most of Europe. However, the spot market dependence also made them vulnerable to volatilities of spot prices under tight market conditions. This was experienced in 1979 when independents were forced to buy expensive supplies on the spot market and resell them at retail prices that, although they barely met the cost, were much higher than the majors' low prices based on cheaper contract supplies.

The interface between the majors and the independents in the retail market provides a useful exposition of the interactions between the spot market and the contract market. These interactions are based on two principles: (a) the relative positions of the average and marginal cost curves under soft versus tight market conditions; and (b) the difference between the weighted average cost of supplies to independents and the majors. These principles, explained below, are the main vehicles through which spot and contract prices interact to bring about an equilibrium price at the retail level. The retail price will then work its way back to the crude level decisions (quantity or price adjustments).

One of the basic tenets in economic theory is that in order for a producer to maximize profits, he should expand or limit production to the point at which the revenue from the sale of the last unit (marginal revenue) is equal to the cost of producing it (marginal cost). Although the oil industry's long-term decisions are guided by this principle, its short-term decisions are much more constrained. An oil company has customers to serve and a market share to protect. Therefore, it cannot change its supply level freely. Yet the marginal cost of supply may change every day, and the company has to do its best to cope with its market obligations while trying to maximize its profit. Figure 1.1 shows the relative positions of average cost and marginal cost curves under soft and tight market conditions. Under soft market conditions, the average cost to each company remains constant up to the level of contracted supplies. This is basically the traditional take-or-pay contract that obliges the company to buy a specified quantity of crude at a contracted price. Beyond the level of contract supply, the company can go to the spot market and buy the additional crude at a cheaper price. Therefore, its marginal cost is below its average cost. As it buys more on the spot market, the average cost of its crude supplies will be reduced but still remain above the cost of the spot crude. Thus, an independent company, which has fewer contract obligations than a major, can acquire its crude supply at a lower average cost by depending more on spot market supplies. Under tight market conditions, the opposite situation would prevail: the marginal supply of crude would be procured on the spot market at a price higher than the contract price.

Based on its mix of spot and contract supplies, and under certain regulatory constraints in most countries, an oil company has to set its retail price high enough to cover its costs and low enough to compete with the retail outlets of other companies. This price would, on the cost side, depend on the weighted average cost of spot and contract supplies. This is true for both major companies and independents. However, the weight is different for each group. The contract price has a higher weight in the case of the majors, while the spot price has a higher weight for the independents. This is the principal vehicle that brings about an equilibrium in the retail market.

For example, if the contract price is substantially above the spot price (soft market conditions), the purchases by independents of spot crude (and products) enable the independents to sell their products at a lower price in the retail market. The majors' cost structure would require selling at a higher retail price, but the majors would have to lower their price in order to preserve their market share. This interface in the retail market would lead to an equilibrium price at the retail level. The resultant retail price would yield a netback value on the basis of which the companies would have to adjust their crude/product purchase policy. The process would eventually affect producers' supply decisions in the form of a change in quantity and/or price. The spot/contract interaction is illustrated in Figure 1.2.

Figure 1.1
Average and Marginal Cost Curves Under Soft and Tight Conditions

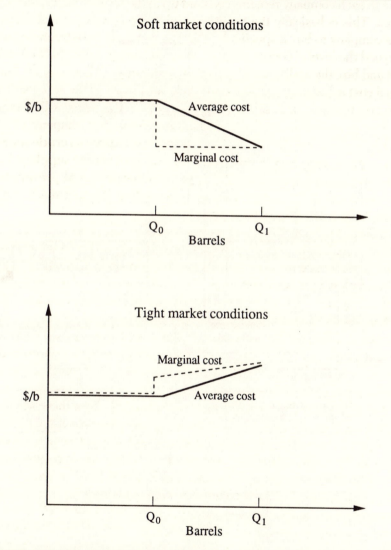

Figure 1.2
How Spot and Contract Markets Interact

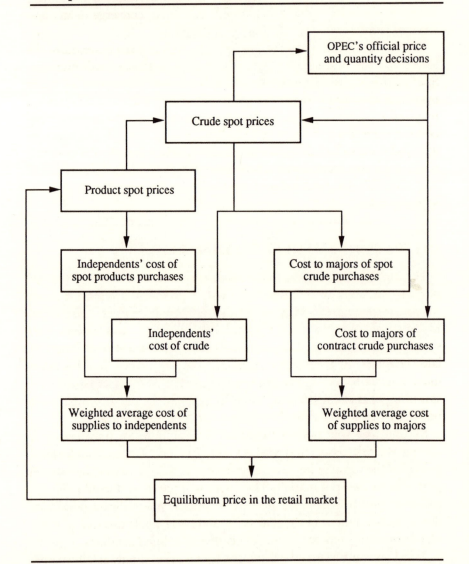

In the past, the separation of the majors' and independents' channels of crude (and products) supplies allowed the spot/contract interaction process to serve as a system of checks and balances. When the gap between contract and spot prices widens, costs to independents and to the majors vary widely. The cost difference is initially reflected in different prices on the retail market that would, over time, converge to an equilibrium price.

In the future, the interaction process will remain essentially the same, but the number of players (or groups of players) will increase. Spot trading is no longer limited to independent oil companies; many majors, state-owned oil companies, and OPEC producers are becoming involved in spot or spot-related trading. As a result, the market is becoming more fluid. The market disequilibriums show themselves rapidly and need to be taken care of equally quickly. That is, the contract/spot interaction mechanism is becoming more efficient as a larger number of entities (on both sides of the trade) are learning how to use the spot market.

INTERACTIONS WITH FUTURES MARKETS

Having developed into a major market, spot trading serves three important functions for the industry. First, it provides information about market clearing prices of crude oil and petroleum products. This information is extensively used by producers, refiners, and traders. The sources and reliability of this information is discussed at some length in later chapters. At this stage it need only be pointed out that this information is not based on comprehensive surveys or even representative sampling of trade activities, since there is no formal administrative body or a physical trading floor to register spot transactions.

Second, the spot market functions as a medium for transferring or sharing the risks associated with price fluctuations. If a stockholder fears a drop in the value of his inventory from a decline in prices, he can sell part of it on the spot market. The buyer will purchase the oil in anticipation of profiting from an increase in prices. A significant portion of the spot transactions of the late 1970s and early 1980s was due to speculative stocking and destocking of crude and refined products.

Third, as was discussed earlier, the spot market is now an alternative channel of oil trade. The volume of spot transactions, especially of crude oil, during the last decade increased sharply. The disruption and tight supply conditions of 1979 forced the purchasers of crude and refined products to learn to use the spot market. The reduced demand of the 1980s, on the other hand, has forced producers to sell their oil on the spot market. Thus, with both sides of the market trading in the spot market, a reversal of the present trend becomes unlikely. Further, there will always be an incentive for one of the two sides to trade on the spot market.

Petroleum futures are likely to take over two of the three important functions of the spot market. These are the price discovery and risk transfer functions, both of which the futures market can perform more effectively than the spot market. Regarding the price discovery function, the petroleum spot market is geographically and organizationally dispersed, making collection of an accurate and representative sample of spot prices difficult, if not impossible. In addition, there are institutional limits to processing and disseminating the collected data, which are treated as privileged information available only to those willing to pay for specialized market services. The information provided by the spot market thus suffers from inherent statistical deficiencies. The futures market, however, is not so constrained. Unlike spot transactions, futures contracts are traded on formally organized commodity exchanges. The transaction data are compiled very rapidly and disseminated almost instantaneously; they are available to the public and there are no institutional barriers to their distribution. The futures market is therefore capable of removing, or at least lessening, the impediments to the flow of information in the petroleum industry. In this respect, spot market price information will lose its significance as the futures market is recognized as a more convenient source of price information.

The risk transfer function of the spot market can also be performed more efficiently by the futures market. Indeed, the risk transfer potential of the spot market has always been less than that desired by the industry. The participants in the spot market are petroleum business agents either directly or indirectly involved in the production, processing, distribution, and consumption of petroleum. They normally try to avoid risk in order to manage a smooth operation. During a soft market period, they want to avoid the risk of capital loss due to a decline in the value of their stock. During a tight market period, they want to avoid the risk of paying too much for supplies. For these agents to avoid risk through spot market trading, there should be enough speculators willing to accept the risk. The majority of these risk takers normally come from outside the industry. However, since spot market transactions require substantial capital and specialization, outsiders are not likely to participate in spot trading. Even if they have the capital, they would not know what quality of petroleum to look for, from whom to buy the oil, where to keep it, and to whom to sell it.

Futures trading removes most of the barriers to the entry of outside speculators in petroleum trading. It provides two important facilities: standardization and impersonality. Futures contracts are standardized with respect to quality, quantity, and location of delivery. Participants do not need to know much about the technical characteristics of petroleum. Also, futures contracts are impersonal in that traders do not need to know who is on the other side of the trade. The clearinghouse of the futures exchange assumes the role of buyer to all sellers and the role of seller to all purchasers of contracts. Furthermore, a trader may participate in a futures market by investing as little as a few thousand dollars.

The facilities provided by the futures market for speculative trading is clarified in chapters 5 to 7. At this stage, it is important to note that the standardization and impersonality of the futures market stimulate the participation of speculators and thereby increase the possibility of transferring the risk. A fully developed futures market would serve this function much more efficiently than the spot market.

The third function of the spot market, to serve as a channel of petroleum supply, cannot be taken over by the futures market because, as is explained in later chapters, futures contracts are not a convenient way to trade petroleum physically. However, the physical supply of petroleum is affected by futures markets in two different ways. First, in the short and medium terms, futures markets provide instantaneous information on prices, which considerably facilitates spot trading. Today, most spot trading in the United States is based on futures prices. Second, in the long term, futures markets, if fully developed, will reduce the scope for spot trading, since futures markets can, in practice, provide all the flexibilities that spot trading can offer. Therefore, both sellers and buyers will be able to return to contract trading as a basis for making investment decisions and use futures markets to preserve flexibility in their business operations. This is, however, dependent on the future worldwide development of petroleum futures markets that cover crude oil as well as major petroleum products.

PART TWO

Petroleum Spot Markets

CHAPTER 2

Mechanics of Spot Trading

HOW IT WORKS

The spot market is not a formal institution. It is an informal worldwide network of personal and professional contacts that facilitates the carrying out of cargo-by-cargo sales and purchases of crude oil and petroleum products. Significant refining or storage centers such as those in Rotterdam, New York, or the Caribbean are likely to be the scene of spot transactions and price quotations, although market participants can be located anywhere, as can the oil traded. The cargo being traded can and usually is already at sea. Participants do not meet to match bids and offers; the transactions take place through telexes of trading offices.

The transaction process has become increasingly complex. In the 1950s and 1960s most of the trade was in the form of uninvoiced exchanges. This was acceptable at a time when only a few companies were involved and trading was based on personal trust. After the oil price hikes of the 1970s, it became impossible to conduct business on such a basis. The cargo became too valuable to be secured by simple trust, which itself became untenable by the entry of numerous small traders. Today, there is very little uninvoiced exchange. Instead, a spot trade involves millions of dollars and is carried out by sale and purchase agreements with a host of safeguard measures. Since a typical cargo of gasoil (i.e., 20,000 to 24,000 tons) is worth about $4 million and a typical cargo of crude may be worth at least $20 million, banks become involved in financing the transaction, insurance arrangements have to be made, and quality and inspection procedures must be defined in detail.

Even so, disputes still arise. The most common are

- Nondelivery or nonlifting—normally in periods of sharp price change based on alleged or real *force majeure*, etc.;
- Delayed delivery;
- Quality disputes and price differentials;
- Inspection disputes;
- Payment disputes; and
- Bankruptcy disputes.

It is difficult to calculate the quantity of petroleum (crude or products) moving through spot channels. Due to multiple exchanges between traders, the volume of trade is always much larger than the amount of oil actually delivered. Each shipment is traded several times before reaching the final consumer, and each time one is traded it is added to the statistics on the volume of trade. A remarkable example of spot trading involved the "daisy chain" trading of a cargo of Brent crude that was traced by *Petroleum Intelligence Weekly* in 1984 (Figure 2.1). The trade involved one cargo of crude oil bought and sold by twenty-four trading entities in thirty-six transactions over a period of three months. The trade for March 1984 delivery started in January. The twenty-four trading entities involved included major international oil companies, national oil companies, refiners, and independent marketers and traders. (From among the majors, Shell appears three times [as Shell U.K., Shell International, and Pecten], British Petroleum [BP] appears twice, and Chevron and Texaco once each. Two national oil companies, the British National Oil Company [BNOC] and Finland's Neste, were also involved, as were four U.S. refiners—Occidental, Sohio, Charter, and the final buyer Sun. Charter's trading affiliate, Acorn, alone accounted for four transactions, and Charter itself, one. U.K. independents Tricentrol and Ultramar also participated, as did the Japanese refiner Idemitsu.) Trader Phibro appears six times in the chain, Transworld and the Shell group three times each, and several others twice.

This example occurred during a time of speculation and probably involved a larger-than-average number of transactions. But the nature of the chain is typical. (Many companies trade a single cargo, and some of the repeaters in the chain do not realize they are trading the same cargo.)

Figure 2.1
"Daisy Chain": Spot Transactions in a Cargo of Crude

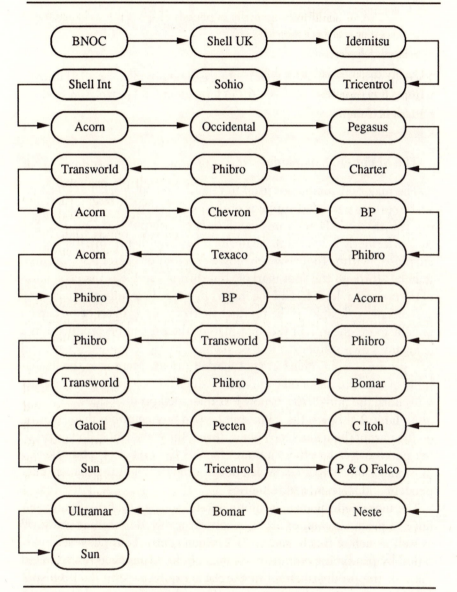

Source: *Petroleum Intelligence Weekly,* November 12, 1984.

MARKET PARTICIPANTS

Majors are becoming traders, the traders are becoming brokers . . . and brokers are becoming journalists.

—*Petroleum Intelligence Weekly*, January 20, 1986

Participants in petroleum spot trading can be broadly classified into: (a) major oil companies (majors), (b) independents, (c) petroleum traders, and (d) brokers.

The Major Oil Companies

The major oil companies used to regard the spot market as a last resort to procure needed supplies or dispose of surpluses. In each refinery run there is always a mismatch between output and demand. The majors formerly balanced these mismatches by either redistributing the surpluses within their own extensive system or correcting the mismatches through the spot market. But during the 1980s the economics of the operation have forced the majors to make their refining/marketing systems more flexible. If the product yield of a barrel of crude oil can be bought more cheaply in the spot market than it can be produced in a company's own refineries, it is economical to reduce refinery runs and buy products from others at spot market prices. Moreover, the availability of crude to major oil companies, which far exceeded their product sales until the mid-1970s, is now less than total product sales.

As Table 2.1 shows, the main shift toward buying rather than refining on the part of the majors took place during the early 1980s. Today, product purchases from others account for 30–40 percent of total sales by most major oil companies. Much of this growth is met by smaller independent and state-owned refineries.

The increased reliance on spot markets by major oil firms is not confined to products. Majors are now actively involved in trading crude oil as well. Much of this began in 1979, when contract supplies were curtailed by producing countries. Majors could either accept a reduced share of the product market or purchase expensive crude on the spot market, refine it, and sell at a loss. They chose the second option. In late 1979, the majors became the biggest buyers in the crude spot market: no other potential buyers had sufficient contract oil at low prices to

Table 2.1.
Growth of Open Market Purchases of Oil Products by Major Oil
Companies, 1978 and 1983 ('000 b/d)

Company	Net purchases		% of total sales	
	1978	1983	1978	1983
British Petroleum	243	555	16	42
Exxon	369	431	18	28
CFP	231	300	22	39
Royal Dutch Shell	24	199	1	15
Mobil	47	107	6	16
Eni/Agip	—	98	—	13
Elf-Aquitaine	—	90	—	20
Chevron	22	84	5	34
Texaco	75	75	12	16

Source: *Petroleum Intelligence Weekly,* October 1, 1984.

support high-priced spot purchases. Immediately after the 1979 crisis, there was a scramble among the majors to secure as much contract crude as possible. As the market softened and spot prices fell below official prices, spot or spot-related purchases of crude became more attractive than term contracts. Today, outside North America, the majors account for about 19 percent of spot trade and acquire 20–30 percent of their crude supplies on a spot basis. The spot share is lower in North America, where most large companies have their own crude supply.

To deal with the changed situation, the majors have set up their own trading affiliates and become involved in complex trading exercises. For example, Shell's trading affiliates are not only involved in spot trading but compete among themselves, and even with Sitco, Shell's central trading unit. Shell has recently split its crude trade activities geographically into Atlantic and Pacific Basin regions. Mobil has reorganized its trading activities to separate the functions of crude and product trading among its subsidiaries.

The Independent Oil Companies

Independents have always played an important role in spot trading. They were to a large extent the driving force behind the creation and growth of spot markets. Unlike the majors, the independents have always depended on the spot markets for much of their needs. Under soft market conditions, this has worked to their advantage. For example, during the slack years between 1975 and 1978 the independents purchased cheap products on the Rotterdam market and undersold the majors' retail outlets in many European countries. However, this dependence became a major disadvantage in 1978–79 when supplies to the independents were cut back as the majors passed on OPEC supply cuts to their third-party customers. The independents were then forced into the spot market and had to buy their supplies at much higher prices than the official prices charged to the majors. Initially, the retail market settled into two price tiers in some European countries. In West Germany, for example, the majors' low prices and the independents' high spot-related prices coexisted in the retail market. As the majors secured more contract oil, they enlarged their market share, squeezing the independents out of the market. The extent of harm to independents, however, varied from country to country. In West Germany, government officials obliged the majors to provide "lifeboat" supplies to independents. In Italy, the independents were badly hurt.

Despite these setbacks and the growth in the number of spot market participants, the independents remain a vital part of the spot market, accounting for about 11 percent of the total spot crude transactions monitored by Petroleum Argus in 1986–87.

Traders

The number of traders involved in the oil business was very small until the late 1960s, when more trading companies entered the field as demand grew and supply diversified. Trader participation became particularly intense after the crisis of 1973–74, since the costs of entry into the industry (basically a telex and telephone) were low and the potential rewards were high. As a result, the number of traders proliferated to more than 300 in the Rotterdam area alone, though the trade was dominated by those with access to crude and products at the same time. During the slack period 1975–78, a large number of these traders went bankrupt. Thereafter, the number of traders has been fluctuating with market conditions.

A trader's basic function is to "take up positions" with regard to crude oil and petroleum products. That is, he contracts to buy or sell real cargoes of oil and is fully responsible and liable for the cargo. Once a trader has taken title to a cargo, he must sell the cargo, exchange it for another cargo, or store the cargo once it reaches the port of delivery. The least risky operation for a trader is a "back-to-back" deal—that is, one in which both seller and buyer have been arranged in advance. In such deals, the trader behaves very much like a broker, buying and selling almost simultaneously. If he foresees a price rise, a trader may buy a cargo without the immediate security of a buyer; by doing so, he would take a "long position." Conversely, when prices are falling, a trader may decide to arrange a sale, without having the oil in his possession, in anticipation that nearer to the date of completion he will be able to purchase the oil at a lower price. This is called "selling short." Some traders may have their crude oil refined and then sell the products partly on the spot market and partly under contract or multicargo arrangements. Finally, some traders take advantage of seasonal demand for heating oil, purchasing it cheaply in the summer, storing it, and selling it in winter when demand and prices are up. The price fluctuations of recent years have made the profitability of seasonal trading more uncertain.

Today, international petroleum trading is concentrated in the hands of a few large reputable trading companies such as Phibro, Marc Rich, Bulk Oil, and Transworld Oil. All these companies account for more than half of the business done by traders. At the local level, a large number of sporadically active traders is involved. These small, peripheral traders enter and leave the business in response to the margins available. When prices are fluctuating, margins widen, motivating more traders to enter the market. When spot product prices rose explosively in 1978, some traders acquired fortunes overnight. But in 1979, when traders were paying greater and greater premiums over current prices to secure scarce cargoes, the spot market turned down—especially in gasoline—and many small traders went bankrupt. When prices stabilized, the volume of trade shrunk, and survival, rather than profit, became the traders' main objective.

Brokers

Brokerage firms are often one-man operations, mostly operating out of London and New York. Many are general brokers for whom oil is only part of their business. Unlike a trader, the broker holds no title to the cargo traded but is a paid go-between who discovers availability or needs and brings together buyers and sellers. Brokers are compensated on a commission basis and are therefore not exposed to the risks involved in price fluctuations. The commission is normally specified in dollars per ton and is paid by the seller.

Brokers are a useful source of market intelligence, since they need good knowledge of the market in order to operate. Also, brokers are occasionally prepared to impart such information in return for a commission. They also have a different relationship with their client than traders do. For the trader, clients are adversaries, since the trader makes his profit by purchasing cheaply and selling dearly at the clients' expense. The broker, on the other hand, operates from a position of neutrality and, as such, is less controversial than the trader.

THE ROTTERDAM MARKET

Spot trading in general is often referred to as the Rotterdam market. This association arose because Rotterdam was the birthplace of petroleum spot trading, which was, in turn, due to its extensive oil production, storage, and distribution facilities. Rotterdam has always been the most active spot market as well as the only market that both imports and exports large quantities of spot crude and products. It also plays a central role in the world spot market. However, any reference to the Rotterdam spot market embraces all spot trading concluded in northwestern Europe—including Sweden, Denmark and Norway, the east coast of England, the Federal Republic of Germany (FRG), the Netherlands, Belgium, and northwestern France. Furthermore, all spot transactions taking place elsewhere in the world, but relating to crude oil or products stored in Rotterdam, or destined for or leaving one of the above countries, are normally regarded as transactions on the Rotterdam market.

Logistically, Rotterdam trade consists of two distinct but related segments:

- An international cargo trade via large oil tankers that takes place between Rotterdam and ports throughout the world, but especially those in the North Sea area; and
- A barge trade from Rotterdam and the Rhine delta to consumers in the Netherlands, West Germany, Belgium, Switzerland, and France.

Rotterdam links these two trade segments together by providing facilities for breaking cargo shipments into barge lots.

Development of the Rotterdam market has been closely related to developments in the petroleum industry itself. Rotterdam first became significant to the oil trade in the early 1960s with the discovery of Libyan crude supplies by U.S. independents. These discoveries represented a substantial source of low-priced crude oil outside the majors' closed system. Barred from the U.S. market by import quotas, this oil was diverted to the large and rapidly growing European market; independent refining and trading of petroleum products was then developing in Europe, particularly at the port of Rotterdam.

Rotterdam's geographic position made it a particularly attractive center for oil trading. Located at the mouth of the Rhine, Rotterdam offered the independents easy access to the hinterland markets in Western Europe as well as to overseas markets. As a deep-water port, Rotterdam could accommodate large oil tankers. Recognizing these attractive features, major oil companies joined the independents by gradually developing their swing refining capacity there. These developments saw the Rotterdam market through its birth and infancy.

The second stage of Rotterdam's development began with the 1973–74 oil embargo and continued until 1978. High petroleum prices and the recession of 1974–75 depressed petroleum demand and left the Rotterdam market with excess capacity in all its operations. At the same time, demand shifted towards lighter products, and the less-sophisticated refineries became unprofitable to operate. The market forced these refineries to run at lower rates of utilization and their operators to meet product shortages (and to dispose of surpluses) in the Rotterdam market. During this period the market was also recognized by the governments of many European countries as a "free" market for petroleum, on which many domestic price control policies could be based.

The third stage of Rotterdam's development began in late 1978, when the market there became recognized as the barometer of global oil demand and supply. At that time, the price of crude moved towards its peak of $40.00 per barrel (b). OPEC and non-OPEC producers began to use information from the Rotterdam market to set increases in prices and justified the increases by the growth in market demand exhibited by Rotterdam prices. Actual trading on the Rotterdam market was very thin, but it was viewed, at least by producing countries, as the only valid reference point for the demand/supply balance. This view was not shared by consumer states, which were irritated by the proposition that such a small portion of total supplies, not even representative of Europe as a whole, could be given such disproportionate importance.

Concern about the effects of high Rotterdam prices on the world economy prompted the governments of industrial countries to seek ways to control the market. The leaders of six major oil-importing countries (the United States, the Federal Republic of Germany, France, Italy, Japan, and the United Kingdom) pledged at the Tokyo Summit in June 1979 to try to moderate Rotterdam market activity. At the same time, the European Commission undertook two separate examinations of the Rotterdam market. The first was the reintroduction of a register of spot transactions that had been carried out for six months in 1978 and termed *Check-Run*. The new register, called *Comma* (Commission Market Analysis), ran from June 1979 to May 1980 with the voluntary participation of the industry. The aim of the new register was to provide a deeper understanding of the Rotterdam market's structure and operation. The second examination, organized by the commission, was undertaken by a group of experts from various parts of the oil industry. Called the "Bourse Group," these experts studied the possibility of establishing a formalized trading floor for oil. The outcome of both examinations was, in effect, an endorsement of the Rotterdam market as a more or less free market for petroleum. The commission decided that neither continuing to monitor spot transactions nor creating a petroleum trading floor was necessary. It should be noted that by the time these investigations were completed prices had softened substantially, and Rotterdam had turned from a sellers' to a buyers' market.

Today Rotterdam is still considered a very important oil trading center of the world, and its prices still represent the reference point for market analysis and many trade agreements. However, Rotterdam is no longer the only important spot market; there are growing spot markets in the United States, the Far East, and the Persian Gulf. In addition, the rapid growth of the futures market in the United States has shifted some attention away from Rotterdam prices to the price of West Texas Intermediate (WTI) crude on NYMEX.

OTHER SPOT MARKETS

Partly in response to growth in spot trading, as well as to other developments in the oil industry, spot markets are growing rapidly worldwide. U.S. spot markets increased in importance after the deregulation of petroleum prices by the Reagan administration in 1981. The Far East markets have become rather well established, and the Persian Gulf markets are expanding quickly. However, the most influential of the growing spot markets are the United Kingdom Brent and the Singapore spot markets.

The Brent Market

The Brent market is a recent development in oil trading. It includes both spot and forward trading. The development of this market took place during 1981–82 in response to a number of factors, the most important of which was the incentive to sell crude oil in advance of its production in order to avoid the risk associated with falling oil prices. At the initial stage, trade was limited to actual oil (wet barrels), even though a specific cargo could have changed hands several times before delivery. By the end of 1982, however, the market expanded to cover a large number of paper deals, which were struck based on the speculating of future prices and which were closed before delivery.

The development of the Brent market was initially due to the coincidence of: (a) the interest among traders to "sell short," and (b) the willingness by a number of oil companies to sell their equity oil in the spot market for tax purposes. The interest among traders to sell short was due to the expectation that crude prices would fall; traders also hoped that they would be able to buy the oil needed to fulfill obligations at a price lower than the price at which the oil had been sold. The oil companies' incentive to sell in the spot market emerged from the fact that, prior to the 1987 revisions in the U.K. tax laws, oil companies were able to pick the lowest-priced cargo from many sales over a period of several months as equity oil on which upstream taxes would be paid. In this manner, oil companies could minimize tax liabilities through multiple buying and selling of their equity crude. There was, therefore, a match of incentives; the trader would sell short and then balance the short-selling with forward sales by the oil companies. In other words, at this stage, short-selling also meant forward selling.

In 1982, short-selling went beyond forward selling of future oil supplies. It instead began to include sales that were not really intended for end users but to be closed before the date of delivery. In this regard the Brent market began to serve as a futures market, although the Brent market is not formally institutionalized and regulated.

The Brent market is frequently called a trading club. There is a limited number of participants, and they all know each other. Contracts are large (500,000 barrels of 38 ° API, low-sulphur Brent Blend) and are negotiated directly between participants. There are no membership requirements, but the ability to enter the actual deal depends on the identity and reputation of the participant. All deals are made verbally and telex confirmations follow. The terms of transactions are not disclosed and not registered anywhere. There is no clearinghouse. Contracts are series of pair-wise deals. Each contract involves a binding commitment to buy (sell) the actual oil and will be executed unless the contract is canceled sufficiently far ahead of delivery time through an explicit "book-out" agreement. Thus, the trading of "paper oil" (i.e., a transaction with no intention of delivery) is much more complicated in the Brent market than in a typical futures market such as NYMEX.

There are two types of transactions in the Brent market: a dated cargo and a fifteen-day cargo. The dated cargo is a sale/purchase agreement for a specific cargo of oil within a specified date range. Thus, it is a spot transaction such as those in Rotterdam or elsewhere. The fifteen-day cargo is a forward transaction. It is a sale/purchase agreement for a cargo of oil to be delivered on an unspecified day of a specified month. Thus, it would not refer to a specific cargo of oil but would only specify, for example, August Brent. The actual delivery date is determined at a later stage by the seller with a minimum notice of fifteen calendar days. (This is how the term *fifteen-day cargo* originated.)

The dated cargo involves a physical transaction in which a specific cargo actually changes hands. The fifteen-day cargo, on the other hand, can be actual or only a speculative deal that would be canceled before delivery. The fifteen-day Brent is traded up to three months ahead of the date of loading. Thus, participants can take short or long positions in the market, buying or selling cargoes of forward months without physical coverage in the first instance. As the month of delivery approaches, the primary seller (a seller who actually has the oil) issues a fifteen-day notice of delivery to his buyer. The buyer, who may not be the end user and who may have sold a contract to another buyer, would issue the same notice to the second buyer. The process continues until someone takes the oil. The fifteen-day requirement is an important condition, and each seller should issue the delivery notice before the fifteen-day deadline. In addition to those traders who get out of delivery obligations by passing the cargo to the next firm in the chain, some participants cancel their obligations to buy (or sell) by agreeing among themselves on a book-out before delivery notices are issued. The book-out takes place based on an agreed reference price, with a cash settlement for the difference between this reference price and the initial sales/purchase price in the contract.

The Brent market played quite a significant role in the petroleum industry during 1982–85 in two distinct ways. First, the Brent market became the industry's own futures market as opposed to other futures markets that were viewed as belonging to commodity traders. Second, the Brent Blend became an important "marker" crude, the price of which was extremely important in reflecting the demand/supply conditions of crude oil. The significance of the Brent market has now somewhat declined due to: (a) revision of the U.K. tax laws in 1987; (b) acceptance and utilization of NYMEX by the oil industry to hedge or speculate on future prices; and (c) increased reliance on NYMEX prices as the market barometer. The new tax laws that took effect on March 1, 1987, oblige oil companies to designate a sale within two days if they wish the transaction to count as the sale of equity oil on which the company has to pay taxes. This removes the incentive to continue selling and buying back paper cargoes many months ahead of delivery in order to achieve the lowest possible sales price for tax purposes. In addition to the revision of the tax laws, the U.K. Financial Services Act, which took effect in October 1987, imposes onerous obligations on companies engaging in "investment" business in the United Kingdom, making Brent potentially less attractive to many speculating participants. The restrictions imposed by the act make it difficult for companies to choose their trading partners or to offer better terms to favored customers. As a result, the Brent market is becoming less attractive to traders and financial houses who participated in this market to take advantage of the flexibilities of an informal and unregulated market.

The trading volume of the Brent market fluctuates with market conditions but has averaged about twenty transactions per day after the 1987 revision of the U.K. tax laws.[1] There are about forty–forty-five physical cargoes loaded per month. Thus, the average number of trade transactions per cargo varies from five to fifteen, depending on the level of speculative activity. The distribution of transactions between spot and forward deals changes with the volume of trade. In the Brent market, deals can be made for the current month or for three or even four months ahead. An analysis of the trade volumes shows[2] that most trade is concentrated in the category of one-month deals. Trade in two- and three-month deals seems to increase when the total volume of trade increases.

Participants in the Brent market come from a population set of about 130 trading entities. About 25 percent of these entities are continually active in the market, while others trade occasionally. From the total number of participants, about 35 percent are integrated oil companies, and 5 percent, including investment firms, are nonintegrated oil companies. The striking feature of the market is, however, the concentration of activity in the hands of a relatively small number of participants. In

1988, the top ten companies accounted for 53 percent of recorded sales, the top twenty, 75 percent, and the top thirty, 87 percent. The ten most active participants included five oil companies and five traders. Among the most active oil companies, BP had the highest profile, while Sun, Gulf, and Shell played important roles in the market. Traders frequently named were Phibro, Transworld Oil, Voest Alpine, Internorth, P&O Falco, and Gatoil.

The Singapore Market

Singapore's central location at the crossroads of Asia has made Singapore the second largest petroleum port of call in the world, next to Rotterdam. With about one million barrels per day (b/d) of nominal refining capacity, Singapore is the world's third largest refining center after Rotterdam and the U.S. Gulf Coast. It has traditionally served as the "balancing" refining center for the Asia-Pacific region, in that it supplies consuming centers when shortages of certain products arise. Singapore's refining activities include (a) conventional operations such as importing and processing crude and selling products on a term or spot basis; (b) term processing—that is, receiving crude from national oil companies (Indonesia's Mindo, Malaysia's Petronas, China's Sinochem, and the United Arab Emirates' Adnoc), processing it, and returning to them all or part of the product yields; and (c) spot processing—that is, receiving crude from traders and returning the refined products to them. An indication of the distribution of activities is given in Table 2.2.

The outlook for Singapore is somewhat mixed. The future of Singapore's refineries is not very bright, since demand for crude processing, which has long been the refineries' main activity, is less now than in the early 1980s. In the face of increasing competition from export refineries in the Middle East, Singapore's refineries now must consider whether to upgrade their facilities by building new, sophisticated units, thus positioning themselves to tap the growing demand for gasoline. At the same time, the outlook for trading in Singapore looks exceptionally good. Because of its history as a major refining center, Singapore has infrastructural services to support large-scale trading in oil. At present, it has over thirty oil trading companies, including subsidiaries of the major oil companies, the national oil companies of OPEC countries, the independent U.S. trading companies, and Japanese trading houses. These companies deal with both on-the-spot and term transactions.

Singapore is in an ideal position to take advantage of trading opportunities. With crude oil imports from all sources totaling more than

Table 2.2.
Singapore Petroleum Processing in 1985/86 ('000 b/d)

Term processing	
Indonesia (Mindo)	30–100
Malaysia (Petronas)	50–65
China (Sinochem)	80–100
UAE (Adnoc)	20
Subtotal	180–285
Spot processing	
Indonesian crude	50–75
Iranian crude	30–50
Subtotal	80–125
Other processing	340–290
Total	600–700

600,000 b/d in 1986 and domestic demand at just 66,000 b/d, about 90 percent of imports were for reexporting (see Table 2.3). Its trading potential is particularly good in view of the following factors:

• The flow of Middle East products into the Asia-Pacific market is rising. Continuing crude oil disposal problems are also pushing Asian producers such as China, Indonesia, and Malaysia into product marketing. As a result, product trading in the Asia-Pacific region is rising, together with opportunities for Singaporean trading companies to expand their region-wide role in product balancing deals.

• The presence of almost all major world oil companies and oil trading organizations allows major decisions on product trading to be coordinated from Singapore.

• The large storage facilities of Van Ommeren and Paktank as well as refiner-owned facilities mean that large-scale product trading can occur.

• A free market economy, as well as excellent telecommunications and other infrastructure, makes Singapore ideally suited to respond to changes in the Asia-Pacific oil market.

• Implementation of the new petroleum price reporting system and possible introduction of a petroleum futures market in Singapore will provide much of the price transparency and market information needed to conduct trade.

Table 2.3
Singapore's Oil Trade in 1986 by Source and Destination

| Imports of crude oil ('000 b/d) | | Exports ('000 b/d) | | | | | | |
Source	Quantity	Destination	Fuel oil	Gasoil	Jet fuel	Naphtha	Gasoline	Kerosene	Total
Kuwait	139	Japan	46	–	30	39	8	8	131
Iran	136	Hong Kong	36	20	16	7	3	5	87
China	129	Malaysia	30	27	4	–	25	2	88
Malaysia	89	United States	25	5	8	1	–	–	39
S. Arabia	50	Australia	10	12	3	1	3	–	29
UAE	44	China	6	21	–	–	–	–	27
Bahrain	–	Philippines	5	–	2	–	–	–	7
Brunei	21	S. Korea	3	–	–	5	–	–	8
United States	–	Thailand	2	32	4	–	–	–	38
Others	19	Iran	–	16	–	–	7	17	40
		Others	10	31	16	7	4	6	74
Total	627	Total	173	164	83	60	50	38	68

Source: Singapore Trade Statistics, 1987.

As oil trading increases in the region, Singapore's trading role will be further enhanced. The emergence of new products from the Middle East flowing to Asia, Europe, and, to a lesser extent, the United States could result in a fundamental realignment of crude and product prices, whereby the movement of Middle Eastern products will be influenced by regional price variations and result in much closer price linkages between the Rotterdam, Singapore, and U.S. (East Coast and Gulf Coast) markets.

CHAPTER 3

Spot-Related Deals

It is difficult to measure the volume of spot trading, since, as indicated in the previous chapter, spot cargoes can be traded many times, leading to inflated reports of the total volume sold in this way. The volume is, nevertheless, measured by various parties that monitor the spot market; the statistics indicate that about 30 percent of crude oil is traded on the spot market. While this still leaves the greater proportion of oil trade as term business, many term trades are agreed to under conditions heavily influenced by the spot market. More and more, term transactions are struck in relation to the spot price prevailing at the time of the deal and allow for price changes during the term of the contract.

A wide variety of mechanisms are used to tie the price of oil to prevailing spot market prices, depending on the circumstances of the buyers and sellers. Such mechanisms include countertrading and various premium and discounting schemes such as package deals, spot-related transactions, and deals with favorable financial terms.

COUNTERTRADING

A countertrade is basically an exchange of oil for goods and services. This type of trade, with an estimated volume of about 2–2.5 million b/d, takes a variety of forms, the most common being barter deals, counterfinancing arrangements, and delivery of oil to settle past debts.

As the name implies, barter transactions include the exchange of oil for a specific set of goods and services. During 1984–86, for example, Saudi Arabia traded oil for ten Boeing airliners and Abu Dhabi received eighteen French Mirage jet fighters. Iran and New Zealand exchanged oil for lambs, while Algeria and Japan traded oil and vehicles. Malaysia and Brazil exchanged oil for ore and Iran and Japan exchanged oil for construction projects, and so on.

In counterfinancing, part of the oil revenues must be used to purchase goods from the oil-importing country. This arrangement is more flexible than a barter deal, because it allows the oil-exporting country to choose all or part of its payment from a wide range of goods and services. Iran has entered into counterfinancing arrangements with a large number of countries, including Austria, Brazil, Greece, Pakistan, Spain, Syria, Taiwan, Turkey, and Yugoslavia. Similarly, agreements between Iraq and Brazil and between Libya and South Korea require the oil-exporting country to receive a certain portion of its oil revenues in the form of goods and services from the oil-importing country.

Facing a squeeze on their oil revenues, some oil-exporting countries have offered to pay part of their past debts in oil. These include debts to other governments as well as to private companies. Iraq, for example, has used oil to pay debts owed to France, Italy, India, and several Japanese companies. Libya has likewise paid past debts to the Soviet Union and Italy.

Countertrade arrangements are not limited to the exchange of oil for other goods, but also take the form of "oil for oil." A notable example of this type of countertrade is Indonesia's term contracts in which Indonesia sold its crude to, and bought Arab Light and petroleum products from, the satellite oil-trading companies that marketed 330,000 b/d of Indonesian crude. Specifically, the arrangement called for the traders: (a) to buy Indonesian crude from Pertamina at the official price; (b) to sell Arab Light crude (required for Indonesian refineries) to Pertamina at the official price; and (c) to sell back to Pertamina the middle distillates from the processing of Indonesian crude at official company postings, which were normally a few dollars above spot prices. This arrangement was particularly useful during the period when the official price was substantially above the spot price. The arrangement enabled Indonesia to move its oil without upsetting the OPEC price structure[3] while effectively selling its crude at $4.00 to $6.00 below the official price.

Countertrade deals can, in theory, be attractive to both sides of the trade. Petroleum-exporting countries can use them to secure a market for their oil and a supply of some critical import items such as food and military equipment; petroleum-importing countries can use them to promote their exports and increase the security of their oil supplies. However, the real incentive for countertrade depends on the conditions of the petroleum market. When the oil market is tight, with spot prices higher than official prices, oil-importing countries insist on countertrade both for its favorable price terms and its self-financing of foreign exchange. Under soft market conditions, on the other hand, oil-exporting countries pursue countertrade arrangements to increase their oil sales by effectively cutting the price. The practice of discounting is, of course, implicit and in many instances quite complicated. The transfer price, on paper, is normally the same as the official price; but the supplier of the goods is permitted to inflate the price of his goods, thus effectively discounting the oil price. The extent of this discount depends on the difference between the official price and the spot market price, since (a) the oil purchaser has the option of buying it on the spot, or, in some instances, of disposing of the oil at spot-related prices; and (b) the oil-exporting country has only one option—to sell the oil on the spot or at spot-related prices.

Countertrade arrangements have not been free of undesirable consequences. Countertrade creates problems for sellers by discouraging conventional term sales and by fostering the belief that ample volumes of cheaper barter crude are available. This was experienced by Nigeria in September 1985 when seven companies, six of them third-party buyers and one a producer, began to phase out official-priced purchases on the ground that countertrade deals offered to other buyers resulted in much cheaper oil.

For buyers, negative consequences are primarily incurred by traders who do not intend to use the oil. Most of these problems are avoided when the purchaser is the government of an oil-importing country that substitutes oil acquired through countertrade for normal supplies. However, in the majority of cases, the buyer is a private or public entity involved in the production of other goods and services and receives the oil as payment for its goods and services. In such cases, the buying entity has problems in disposing of the oil after receiving it due to a drop in price between the time the countertrade agreement was signed and the time the oil was delivered.

An interesting example of buyers' problems is the Voest Alpine case. Voest Alpine, the Austrian state steel company, had countertrade agreements with Nigeria and Iran to receive their oil at the prevailing official prices. To lessen the risk of a market price movement, Voest had taken short positions on Brent's forward market. The Nigerian coup and consequent review of barter policy put a stop to Nigerian countertrade in the second half of 1985. At the same time, Iraqi air attacks prevented oil exports from Iran. The delay in liftings resulted in a loss of about $65–70 million. Meanwhile, short positions in the forward market were held open in expectation that oil prices would fall sharply in late November or early December. However, Austrian public discussion of this "gambling" with taxpayers' money forced Voest to liquidate the positions just as the market was peaking in November at around $30.00/b. If these positions had been kept open for another ten days, when prices fell by $3.50–4.00/b, they would have yielded a profit of $25 million. Held open a further three months, they would have yielded a profit of $120 million. The lesson from this case is that countertrade arrangements become very difficult to administer under fluctuating prices and unstable political environments.

DISCOUNTS AND PREMIUMS

Discounting or adding a premium to the official price of oil was originally a price adjustment practiced by major oil companies; the majors would lift the oil at the official price and sell part of it to third-party customers at a discount or premium depending on market conditions. In 1977 and early 1978, when the market was weak, oil companies were forced to sell crude to contract buyers at substantial discounts off official prices. In 1979, when the market had picked up, companies began to charge premiums of about 10–20 percent a barrel in the form of shorter credit terms, and "service fees" of $0.05 to $0.50/b. These premiums on oil company sales were increased to more than $8.00/b in a matter of months.

This practice encouraged OPEC governments to seek similar premiums in return for guaranteeing future oil supplies. Despite the statement by the then OPEC president Ali al-Otaiba, "It's the buyer who offers us much higher than OPEC prices . . . please don't offer us higher prices than we demand,"[4] OPEC member countries actively sought premiums on their crude supply. The trend began with Nigeria and Iraq. In mid-1979 Nigeria asked its long-term contract agents to pay for half of their liftings at spot prices (giving an effective premium of $6.00/b); and Iraq required new contract customers to pay a $10.00/b premium payable in advance as a lump sum, nonrefundable "signature bonus." Before the end of the year, the practice had spread to almost all OPEC members as they started to charge premiums in the form of "exploration fees," "compensation for retroactivity," etc. Even non-OPEC members followed the same strategy. The British National Oil Company (BNOC) adopted a surcharge of $3.00/b in January 1980, just a few days after it had raised its official price from $26.00/b to $30.00/b.

The trend toward higher premiums came to an end after the first quarter of 1980. It initially took the form of deductions in the amount of the premium, but by the end of 1980 premiums began to disappear altogether. In mid-1981, buyers began to ask for discounts, and in response Iran cut the price of its light crude by $1.00/b. Other producers gradually adopted the practice, although they often disguised the discount in the form of favored credit terms, package deals, processing deals, etc.

Discounts became very prevalent in 1985–86 and played an important role in breaking OPEC's price structure. Discounts were offered by all producing countries in a variety of forms including direct (temporary) discounts, package deals, transportation and delivery allowances, and favorable financial terms. Direct discounts are, clearly, the easiest to detect. They were initially discounts off the official price, but later they became discounts below the spot market price. Direct discounts also took the form of differentials charged on nonmarket crudes, which were less than those prescribed by OPEC. Package deals are more difficult to trace; both the volume of oil involved and the magnitude of the discount are often unclear. Packaging can be offered in one or a combination of the following forms:

- Packaging officially priced crudes with crudes that are not priced by the OPEC conference or with the equity crude that is fictitiously priced;
- Employment of incentives such as parallel lifting of specific volumes of petroleum products or condensates at low prices, taking advantage of the fact that refined products and condensates are outside the mandate of the OPEC conference; and
- Packaging crude oil with liquefied petroleum gas (LPG), liquefied natural gas (LNG), and petrochemical products.

Transportation and delivery allowances are made either in the form of a direct (per barrel) freight subsidy or by absorbing the cost, indirectly, in one of the following forms:

- Selling the crude on a cost and freight (C + F) or cost, insurance, and freight (CIF) basis, with fictitiously low freight and insurance rates;

- Disposing of the crude at a terminal nearer to the buyer's refinery, thereby granting the buyer a discount on official free on board (FOB) prices; and

- Transporting the crude to the buyer's facilities and actually paying storage fees to the buyer; payment for the crude is made thirty days from the date of actual use by the buyer. In this case, storage is hypothetical, and the date of use is fixed to allow the refiner free credit and greater liquidity.

The provision of a discount by granting favorable financial terms occurs quite often. The most frequent practice in this regard is to extend the credit period of the buyer to two or three months from the normal thirty days. Other forms of favorable financial terms are interest-free or low-interest loans to buyers covering all or part of the shipment; long-term loans, extending over ten years, to finance crude shipments; and noninvoiced quantities delivered together with quantities sold at official prices, thereby effectively granting the buyer a discount.

TERM CONTRACTS WITH SPOT PRICES

The link between term contract prices and crude spot prices is either implicit or explicit. An implicit link refers to term contracts with weekly, monthly, or quarterly renegotiable prices. An explicit link is established through a specific price formula, included in term contracts, which relates the contract price to *Platt's* spot price (monthly, fortnightly, or weekly) averages.

Implicit links have, in one form or the other, been part of term contracts since the early 1980s. Iran was the first producing country to begin this practice on a large scale. In the first quarter of 1982, Iran signed several contracts with European buyers for six- to nine-month terms, under which prices were set each month on what was virtually a spot level. By May 1982, Iran offered some Japanese buyers quarterly deals at prices set ten days ahead of each quarter.

The practice of either implicit or explicit term/spot price linkages was begun in 1984 by Norway's Statoil Company. In December 1984, Statoil and its term customers agreed to settle the price of volumes lifted in each month at the end of that month, in light of open market trends. This could be a single price, or if the spot market fluctuated widely, cargo-by-cargo pricing based on the date of nomination of loading. Seven months later, Mexico followed suit by using "market-responsive" prices in its term contracts. Mexico had always adhered to its official prices, but this adherence had cost it almost half of its market share.

The market-responsive price mechanism was chosen as a way to redirect exports back to the target of 1.5 million b/d.

By mid-1986, spot-related term contracts became common. North Sea producers effectively abandoned the concept of setting a fixed "official" contract price. Iran was selling about 300,000 b/d to Japanese firms under so-called frame contracts, which linked prices to spot market quotations. Iraq was selling about 200,000 b/d of Basrah Light crude to Japanese buyers based on average spot prices of Dubai, Oman, and Arab Light in equal proportions, less the freight differential. Saudi Arabia was selling products from its new refineries at spot-related prices. Other OPEC members, in particular Nigeria and Libya, were involved in similar practices. Even Canadian crudes, which for twelve years had been sold at state-determined prices, were sold at spot-related prices. (The Canadian system is similar to that in the United States: instead of a seller's official price, there is a buyer's posted price, which is kept in constant relationship with spot market prices.)

The spot-related term contracts are not without problems, however. These problems arise because of a big debate over which markets provide the best indication of basic trends for specific crudes and products, and which source of published prices provides the most reliable information. While the debate over which market to choose continues, some consensus seems to be emerging. For the price of crude oil, most attention is now focused on the North Sea Brent, West Texas Intermediate, and the Dubai markets. For refined products, Rotterdam is influential in gasoil and naphtha pricing, the United States is influential in gasoline, heating oil and low-sulphur fuel, and countries east of the Suez are influential in distillates and fuel oil.

The growing need for price information is prompting producers and oil companies to search for "unbiased" market indicators. This has enhanced the influence of the futures market and the spot price reporting of various print and electronic services. The reporting services relied upon in the past have rapidly expanded from traditional sources such as *Platt's Price Service, Petroleum Information Weekly, Petroleum Argus,* and *Oil Buyer's Guide* to include a host of others such as *Reuters, Tolerate, Petroflash, Oil Market Trends,* and the industry-sponsored *Asian Petroleum Price Index.* To minimize the risk of manipulation, some deals rely on a basket of quotes from various published sources and are tied to spot price quotes over a number of days before and after loading or arrival. Price information pitfalls are most pronounced for the secondary crudes and products not actively traded every day. In the ab-

sence of adequate data, selling prices are usually calculated from the
best comparable market, with an agreed link or index to another oil or
location.

Tenders

Short-term tenders for the purchase and sale of crude oil and refined
products are an increasingly popular adjunct to spot-related prices,
both in the industrialized and developing countries. The U.S. government buys roughly 550,000 b/d on tender for use domestically and overseas (for civilian and military needs), plus varying amounts for the Strategic Petroleum Reserve. Other countries, such as Japan, also purchase
stockpile oil, running about 50,000 b/d through tender offers. In the developing world, there are numerous cases of oil tendering, such as in
India, Taiwan, Thailand, Bangladesh, Tanzania, Madagascar, etc. The
buying policy of the Ceylon Petroleum Company of Sri Lanka is a good
example. While retaining term contracts with Saudi Arabia, Iraq, and
Malaysia, Ceylon buys around 20,000 b/d of crude, or about 60 percent
of its total requirements, through tender offers. It also tenders for all its
product sales or purchases, inviting twenty to thirty selected oil companies and traders to offer crude oil about once every six weeks.

NETBACK PRICING CONTRACTS

Netback pricing of term contracts was first practiced by Libya and
Iran in the early 1980s for limited volumes of sales and limited periods
of time. In 1986, netback pricing became much more significant because: (a) for a limited period of time, it replaced OPEC's official pricing scheme; and (b) it provided the oil-producing countries with a price-
war weapon, which was sought by some OPEC members. Netback pricing was practiced on a much more limited scale thereafter, but it could
reemerge whenever oil-producing countries disagree on a coordinated
production and pricing policy. It is therefore very useful to analyze the
consequences of the 1986 netback pricing experience and to assess the
impact it has had on market participants within and outside OPEC.

In 1982, when the market began its downward trend, Saudi Arabia,
which felt somewhat responsible for flooding the market during the period 1979–81, voluntarily reduced its level of production from 9.9 to 6.5
million b/d. In March 1983, it accepted an implicit production quota of

5 million b/d[5] and, more importantly, proclaimed itself OPEC's swing producer. In this latter role, Saudi Arabia was forced to reduce its output to about 2.3 million b/d by the third quarter of 1985. Unhappy with its less powerful position in OPEC, Saudi Arabia announced in July 1985 that it was abandoning the role of swing producer and would try to boost production to a minimum of 3.5 million b/d. Saudi officials, realizing that customers would only be attracted by market-responsive prices, considered three options on which to base their sales price: the Arab Light spot price, the spot prices of other crudes, and the spot prices of refined products. The relatively small amount of Arab Light traded on spot made contracts linked to its spot price unattractive. As for the spot prices of other crudes, North Sea Brent was considered, but this would have meant linking production and pricing policies to a very volatile spot market. Netback value pricing was therefore chosen by process of elimination.

Saudi Arabia's drive to recapture its market share through netback deals was quite successful, and large segments of lost markets in the Atlantic basin and east of Suez were won back. By the first quarter of 1986, its output increased to about 4.5 million b/d, even though it was more interested in consolidating sales to established customers than in dramatically raising exports. This was accomplished by converting existing Petromin contracts at official prices into new netback deals. Most Saudi customers, such as BP, Elf, CFP and Neste, as well as Taiwan's CPC and South Korea, switched from Petromin term contracts to netback deals. Table 3.1 shows estimates of Saudi Arabia's netback contracts in early 1986.

CALCULATION OF NETBACKS

Calculation of netback value aims at deriving a value for crude oil by deducting from the revenue obtainable from selling the refined products the costs of refining and transportation. Since product prices and the yield pattern of refined products vary between crudes and between markets, the calculation needs to be specific to crude and to refinery location.

Figure 3.1 illustrates the concept and the computation mechanism of netback value. The computation is based on the physical movement of oil, which is from port of loading to the ship, from the ship to the refinery, and from the refinery to market. Netback value computation follows these same movements but in reverse order, as follows:

Table 3.1
Saudi Arabia's Netback Contracts in 1986 ('000 b/d)

Western destinations

Majors West	1,070	Europe	425	Americas	235
Exxon	340	Motor Oil Hellas	125	Petrobras	75
Texaco	200	Neste	50	Champlin	60
Mobil	180	Garrone	50	Ashland	50
Chevron	100	Saras	50	Marathon	50
Shell	100	Cepsa	50		
BP	100	Enpetrol	50		
CFP/Elf	50	Turkey	50		
Subtotal West					1,730

Eastern destinations

Majors East	450	Other East	230	Japan	220
Caltex	250	Bahrain	100	Mitsubishi	100
Mobil	100	Taiwan	60	Kyodo	70
Exxon	100	South Korea	50	Marubeni	50
		Pakistan	20–35		
Subtotal East					900
Total					2,630

Source: *Petroleum Intelligence Weekly,* February 10, 1986.

(a) First, the weighted average value of the refined product obtainable from a barrel of crude oil at the refinery gate is computed. The result is known as the gross product worth (GPW) of the crude. It is calculated by multiplying the prevailing spot price for each product by its percentage share in the yield of one barrel of crude oil.

(b) Then, the cost of refining, which consists of the out-of-pocket operating expenses involved in the handling of the last barrel of crude by a refiner, is deducted from the GPW to arrive at the net product worth (NPW) of the crude. Since the marginal barrel is under consideration, this result does not include any amortization or depreciation.

(c) Finally, the cost of transportation and insurance is deducted from the NPW to arrive at the netback value of crude at the port of loading. The transport cost is the cost of chartering an appropriately sized tanker on the spot market for a single voyage.

Figure 3.1
A Netback Value Calculation

Physical movement of oil

| Crude is loaded at the port of loading | → | Crude is shipped to refinery | → | Crude is refined into petroleum products | → | Products are sold ex-refinery at wholesale spot prices |

Computation of netback value

Take the spot price of refined products ($/b)

LPG = 27.80
gasoline = 16.80
heating oil = 23.10
fuel oil = 16.10

Average spot prices in mid-March 1986

Multiply the spot prices by proportionate yields of each product ($/b)

10% LPG × 27.80 = 2.78
42% gasoline × 16.80 = 7.06
20% heating oil × 23.10 = 4.62
24% fuel oil × 15.10 = 3.62
4% lossess = 0
GWP = 18.08

Deduct the cost of refining ($/b)

18.08
-0.45[a]
NPW = 17.63

Deduct the cost of transportation ($/b)

17.63
-1.85
15.78

The result is the netback value of crude at the port of loading

$15.78/b

[a]Note: Saudi netback deals include an allowance of $1.50 to $2.00/b for capital costs. Therefore, the average refinery cost is estimated at $2.20/b (consisting of $1.75/b capital cost and $0.45/b operating cost). The above computations for Saudi netback contracts are: NPW = 18.08 − 2.20 = 15.88; and netback value at the port of loading = 15.88 − 1.85 = 14.03 $/b.

The logic of calculating the netback value at the port of loading should now be clear. By subtracting refining and freight costs, spot product prices are translated into an equivalent crude oil value at the port of loading—the so-called FOB netback. Thus, if the price of crude is supposed to be determined by the netback value, the logical choice would be to relate the FOB price of the crude to the FOB netback value at the port of loading.

There are a few points worth noting in the netback calculation procedure. First, the most important information in this calculation is the refinery yield—that is, the mix of products obtained from a barrel of crude oil. This mix varies not only with the quality of each crude, but also with the pattern of local market crudes—which can shift from winter to summer—and with the technical capabilities of individual refineries. Thus, looking for specific yield patterns would require compiling thousands of mixes corresponding with various crudes, various refineries, and different periods. Recognizing the impossibility of such a task, the *Petroleum Intelligence Weekly* has developed data on crude oil yield patterns that are typical or representative of the refining industry in each of the six major refining centers.

Second, the refining cost, used in netback value calculations, does not include capital costs. The implication is that netback value is purely a marginal phenomenon that corresponds with the short-term operation of a refinery. Thus, netback value is not intended to provide a basis for long-term development and resource management.

Saudi Arabia's netback pricing contracts followed the general concept described above, but, instead of limiting the refining cost to "out-of-pocket" operational expenses, Saudi contracts allowed for some ($1.50–2.00/b) capital cost. Thus, the total refining (operational and capital) cost could be as high as $2.00–2.50/b.

As to the mechanics of the trade, the buyer was responsible for refining the crude. Product prices were based on the average (between the date of loading and date of discharge) of *Platt's* price series and corresponded to the location of the refinery where the buyer would run the crude. In the soft markets of mid-1986, purchasers insisted on paying according to the spot prices of the latest possible date. Some contracts were based on the spot prices that fell within five or ten days of the date of discharge, or they were based on relatively long periods (twenty-five days) after the date of loading. The freight and insurance allowance was based on actual costs for each cargo.

Saudi netback contracts with the Far East were in some respects different from those with the West. First, pricing was based on an average of product prices near the date of lifting, while contracts for Western destinations were linked to prices at the time of discharge. Second, Far East deals were based on Rotterdam prices, due to thin trading in local spot markets, with freight deducted from Ras Tanura. An extra $0.60/b was then charged to compensate for the lower freight costs that prevail to the East as well as historically higher prices there. Third, fuel oil yields in the contracts with Japan were less than those in contracts with the U.S. oil companies, although the average fuel oil yield in Japan was much higher than in the United States.

Saudi netback contract provisions set an example for other producers to follow. In January 1986, Nigeria signed netback contracts with its equity partners, guaranteeing them a minimum $2.00/b margin on their own share of crude and $1.00/b on government oil. These contract arrangements were similar to Saudi netback sales except for one important difference: the Nigerian price was based on an average of published product prices in the calendar month in which each crude cargo was lifted. Saudi contracts were based on the average price around the date of discharge. In the Nigerian contract, the refining cost allowance per barrel was $1.80 for the U.S. Gulf Coast, $1.30 for northwestern Europe, $1.20 for the Mediterranean, and $1.00 for the Caribbean.

Iran's netback contracts were also similar in structure to Saudi Arabia's, but had an additional feature—a floor and ceiling mechanism. A formula tied to spot crude prices defined the limits within which netback pricing applied. If the netback value went above or below these limits, the spot crude formula was used instead. Thus, if netback values fluctuated too widely out of line with the spot crude market, they were disregarded, protecting both buyer and seller. The spot crude formula was based on an average of Brent and Dubai prices, with the "floor" about $2.00 below and the "ceiling" about $1.00 above.

CONSEQUENCES OF NETBACK DEALS

Netback pricing transfers the market risk from downstream operations to the producer. It also transmits a price signal from the heart of the market to the producer.

The risk transfer role is valued very highly by oil companies. In a falling market, oil companies can incur substantial losses from price declines between the date they buy the crude at the port of loading and the date they sell the refined products manufactured from that crude. They are therefore interested in avoiding as much of this risk as possible. Some oil companies have begun to use the futures market for this purpose. They can sell short on the futures market around the same date when they buy the oil at the port of loading, and liquidate the position around the time they sell the products. The futures market, however, does not provide complete protection since it does not cover various crudes, various products, and various locations.

Netback contracts with a pricing date close to the date when the products are sold provide a more convenient way of transferring risk. An even better arrangement in this regard would be the so-called realization contracts under which the producer sells crude at realized product prices.

The second function of netback pricing—that is, the transmission of price signals—is more neutral. It does not favor either side of the trade but helps both sides to arrive at a common understanding of market conditions. Finding relevant price signals has always been a potential area of dispute between producers and oil companies; netback pricing provides a vehicle for the automatic transmission of price signals.

While serving the above two functions, netback deals should not, in theory, cause any significant change in the structure of the market. In practice, however, these deals have had important consequences for Saudi Arabia, for OPEC, and for the world oil market.

The advantages to Saudi Arabia of netback deals over sales at crude spot prices were more stable price patterns and more reliance on integrated oil companies over traders. On the other hand, these transactions had some severe drawbacks for Saudi Arabia, compared with official sales and crude spot sales. The most important disadvantage was a potential loss of revenue, since netback values tended to be lower than spot and official prices of crude oil, the agreed yields tended to favor buyers, and the refining costs were somewhat excessive.

The reason that crude spot prices stay above the netback value is that the average value of crude for refiners in each market is above the netback value. The spot crude price is an indicator, produced by the market, of the average value of a crude; the netback value is an indicator, worked out by industry specialists, of its marginal value. A negative margin between the netback value and the spot price prevails occasionally. This does not mean, however, that refiners have been consistently bearing losses. Thus, for Saudi Arabia, netback contracts caused a loss by forcing the Saudis to sell at netback rather than at spot prices. The loss was exacerbated by including in the refining cost an allowance for capital costs, which reduced the price paid for its crude to a level below normal industry estimates of its netback value.

In addition to the above areas of potential loss to Saudi Arabia was the refinery yield, or mix of product output, included in Saudi netback contracts. The contracts with U.S. oil companies were based on yields of approximately 40 percent gasoline, 20 percent distillates, 30 percent fuel oil and 10 percent other (LPG and refinery losses). The fuel oil percentage was crucial. Allowance for 30 percent fuel oil in the netback contract with some sophisticated refineries, which normally produce less than 10 percent fuel oil, would in effect discount the value of crude by about 5 percent.

In short, netback contracts had their drawbacks for Saudi Arabia. They undervalued the crude by pricing it at its marginal rather than its average value, by allowing additional refining costs, and by allowing a high proportion of residual fuel oil in the notional slate. In return for the loss of revenue, netback contracts ensured the attractiveness of Saudi crude at a time of oversupply and reestablished Saudi Arabia in the international petroleum market.

Also, by virtue of their provisions, netback pricing deals encouraged oil companies to increase throughputs and sales of products on the spot market. As explained previously, netback contracts cover all operating and some capital costs. Thus, as long as a refiner has excess capacity he will gain from increasing his utilization rate. Furthermore, by basing the netback on product spot prices around the time of product sale, business risk to refiners is low and market conditions at the time of sale will be of little concern. This strategy can further prompt expansion of throughput. Aggregating this behavior over all the oil companies results in increased demand for OPEC oil and the flooding of the product spot markets with direct or indirect sales of the additional refinery throughputs. This was actually observed in 1986 when netback pricing became commonplace and the netback value as well as the spot price of crude oil dropped below $10.00/b.

CHAPTER 4

The Role of Petroleum Spot Prices

SOURCES OF INFORMATION

All trading needs market information, or striking a bargain with any confidence becomes impossible. In petroleum trading this information is provided through business contacts, to which can be added information published by such services as *Platt's Oilgram*, *Oil Buyers' Guide*, *Petroleum Argus*, *Petroleum Intelligence Weekly*, and some other sources.

Platt's Oilgram was founded in the 1920s to report on prices in Texas and in the U.S. Gulf Coast. In the 1960s, *Platt's* began a European price series, which was in 1966 converted to the current Rotterdam price information. In 1970, *Petroleum Argus* began in London. More recently, daily price information became available through the international press agencies Reuters, AP/Dow Jones, and Petroflash. Petroflash was initially established as a joint venture by *Petroleum Intelligence Weekly* and *Oil Buyers' Guide* but was acquired by McGraw Hill, the publisher of *Platt's*, in 1985.

All these price sources share certain properties: the prices they publish are based on regular trawlings of market information and not on comprehensive formal surveys or even representative samplings of actual price quotations. *Platt's*, the most influential source of price data, has developed a network of contacts—traders, brokers, and refiners (all of them deemed to be active in the trade)—from which information on the spot market is collected daily. From this information, the *Platt's* staff prepares what it calls an "assessment" of spot prices. The quotations are not reports of the extreme limits but are assessments of the day's prices for "typical" or "generally available" products. These assessments, unavoidably, contain some subjective elements. The subjectivity surfaces in a number of ways. For example, the spot price series tend to lag behind large price changes in the market. Assessors are reluctant to validate large price changes, even when the statistical average of reports would encourage them to do so. Instead, prices are increased in small shifts as the trading community's reaction is tested. Nevertheless, the information is considered useful. It complements the traders' judgment of market conditions. As one expert describes the situation, "The process of collecting scraps of information and piecing together an impression of the whole is exactly what any trader does himself when evaluating the market. A (*Platt's*) journalist may have a better chance of putting together an accurate picture, since he can cast his net more widely."[6]

USES OF SPOT PRICES

Use of spot prices reported by organizations such as *Platt's* is much wider than might be expected. The primary areas of use are

- Product term contracts with variable pricing clause;
- Crude oil sales based on spot crude or product prices;
- Management of refining/marketing activity;
- Adjustments in refineries' posted prices; and
- Government retail price controls linked to spot product prices.

There are two ways by which product term contracts between refiners and marketers are normally related to the spot price. Either there is an explicit linkage through the inclusion of a formula that automatically changes the contract price as spot prices vary, or there is a de facto linkage through the inclusion of a periodic price review clause, which would normally provide for monthly or quarterly renegotiation of the price based on spot market trends. Both of these arrangements may result in contract prices that somewhat lag behind the spot price, but the influence of the spot price would in any event remain substantial.

Crude oil sales based on spot prices are of more recent origin. They take the form of

- Term contracts with an automatic price adjustment;
- Term contracts with a monthly or quarterly renegotiation clause;
- Netback value contracts; and
- Realization deals.

These arrangements are discussed in chapter 3.

The use of product spot prices in the management of refining/marketing activity is a product of market conditions in the 1980s. For several years, refiners in the United States, Japan, and Western Europe were plagued by overcapacity. Poor operational economies stemming from low capacity utilization, coupled with marginally refined and therefore cheap surplus products available on the spot market, meant that some refining/marketing companies had to consider the possibility of cutting back on running crude themselves, opting instead to buy products manufactured by others. Spot prices were studied closely to determine how much of these companies' needs should be produced through the companies' own refineries and how much should be purchased on the spot market. This practice has now become a routine function of most refining/marketing companies.

The use of product spot prices in setting "posted prices" has also become a normal practice. The posted price is an official selling price set by refiners. Posted prices have traditionally lagged behind product spot prices, which could imply that there is no strong link between posted and spot prices. The catch, however, is that posted prices are not necessarily the prices at which trade occurs. They serve as a reference point for negotiations and, depending on market conditions, there will always be premiums and discounts to account for. These premiums and discounts, on the other hand, take account of the prevailing difference between the posted and spot prices, effectively linking the purchase price to the spot price.

The use of spot prices in government retail price controls emerges from: (a) the need to regulate domestic prices; (b) the need to set a reference point for internal price transfers of integrated oil companies; and (c) the lack of any other measure that could be used for these purposes.

As a result, most European countries have worked out quite complex formulas to relate price maximums and minimums to *Platt's* prices.

MOST FREQUENT COMPLAINTS AGAINST SPOT PRICES: POLITICAL AND TECHNICAL

Complaints against spot prices are of two types: political and technical. Political objections are normally raised when spot prices are moving against the interest of a group. The use of spot prices to support political objectives is clearly demonstrated by the periodic shifts of the position and attitudes of consuming governments and OPEC members towards the legitimacy of spot markets. During the slack years 1974–78, governments of consuming countries used low spot prices as a lever against OPEC price increases and as a medium to limit the majors' domestic prices. OPEC was then playing down spot prices, denouncing their reliability, accuracy, and representativeness. In 1979 consuming governments and OPEC switched positions on the validity of spot prices. OPEC used high spot prices, either explicitly or implicitly, to raise its contract prices. Consuming governments, on the other hand, denounced spot prices as "no longer an indication of overall commercial oil value"[7] and embarked upon various studies to limit the activity of the spot market. As market conditions later reversed, consuming nations again discovered that spot prices represent the true value of oil, while OPEC blamed spot prices for the instability of the petroleum market.

Technical objections to spot prices are more systematic and worth noting. The most frequent complaints are: (a) the lack of an organized trading floor, (b) the thinness of trading, and (c) the inefficient assessing of spot prices.

Lack of an Organized Trading Floor

A point often made about spot prices is that, without a formal trading floor, information on spot prices is necessarily incomplete and unreliable. Because spot trading does not take place on an organized exchange or trading floor, there is no location at which all the deals are made, no registration of membership, no official reporting of transactions (price and volume), and no formal administrative body. Instead, deals are individually registered between agents who can be anywhere. Much of the assessment of these deals is made through *Platt's* editors' telephone calls to selected trading contacts. Therefore, market information is not and cannot be collected within a solid and systematic framework. This is a generally accepted problem in the transparency of present spot prices. The source of the problem lies not, however, in *Platt's* price reporting system, but in the structure of the spot market.

Thin Trading

Thin trading and lack of adequate and continuous supply have occasionally been cited as fundamental problems with spot prices in general, and with *Platt's* assessments in particular. If *Platt's* cannot discover any deals to report, then it repeats the previous day's prices. For some products in certain markets it is not uncommon to have gaps of up to several weeks between publicly reported deals. Thus, when *Platt's* can again report a firm price it may well bear little relation to the one that has been continually restated over the preceding weeks. A prominent example of this is the 1985–86 trend of Arab Light's spot price. *Platt's* assessment of the Arab Light spot price remained at $27.00/b during the collapse of the oil market (November 1985–February 1986), when the price of WTI and Brent plummeted from around $30.00 to $15.00/b.

Oil companies have, during slack periods, extended the thin trading argument to claim that the spot market is, in general, too thin and limited in actual supplies to provide a basis for pricing of petroleum products in retail markets. This is, in nature, a more fundamental criticism than the reporting problem discussed above. However, this complaint indicates a lack of understanding of the role of the spot market. By definition, spot prices are predicated upon marginal transactions, and significant volumes need not be behind such prices. At any point in time, incremental additions to or disposals of one's oil stocks via spot purchases or sales will have different values to different parties. Spot purchases will always be made by the buyer who places the highest value on incremental supplies. Similarly, spot sales will always be made by the seller who least values his excess supplies. Consequently, spot prices show the equilibrium point of the marginal values of oil to the seller and buyer. These prices will almost always be different from the average market prices. What oil companies are pointing out is that the marginal price should not be replacing the average price, which is presumably related to the cost of refining and marketing the oil.

Subjectivity of *Platt's* Price Assessments

Objections to *Platt's* methodology are primarily concerned with the subjectivity of its price assessments. *Platt's* subjectivity is to be expected. Such private endeavors often lack a comprehensive database, and what is missing in statistical data must be filled in by the assessor's intuition about the market. *Platt's* makes no pretensions about this point. It emphasizes that its prices are assessments of market conditions. Nevertheless, the subjectivity in performing these assessments poses problems. For one, no two individuals are ever likely to judge the market precisely the same. How big a problem this subjectivity of assessment is depends on the ways and means in which the prices are used. The traditional role of *Platt's* prices—that is, to provide a feel for the market—is not severely jeopardized by subjective assessments. In fact, some defenders of *Platt's* argue that its assessment is more useful than a huge volume of hourly fluctuating numbers, which a "more objective" statistical compilation of data would provide. But the main objections to the subjectivity issue arise when *Platt's* prices are used as actual market prices in areas such as government price regulations and contract price arrangements, for which *Platt's* prices were not initially intended.

IS THERE AN ALTERNATIVE?

Whenever so much hinges on sets of numbers whose accuracy is subject to question, all ways of improving them are likely to be explored. Efforts in this direction have intensified since the mid-1970s and fall into the following general categories:

- Development of registration/monitoring system;
- Introduction of spot price indices;
- Creation of a formal trading floor; and
- Introduction of futures markets.

Register/Monitoring Systems

Complaints about the inaccuracy and unrepresentativeness of spot prices are to some extent related to the self-interest of those raising them, but to a larger extent they reflect concerns about the problems inherent in the structure of the spot market and the nature of the reporting systems. To evaluate these complaints, the European Commission set up a six-month price monitoring system (Check-Run) in 1978, followed by another (Comma) in 1979–80.

The purpose of Check-Run was to verify published spot quotations—in particular, those of *Platt's Oilgram* Price Service—and cross-check with the actual spot price. Thirty-three companies and a number of traders participated. Of the seven products traded on the spot market (premium and regular gasoline, naphtha, jet kerosene, gasoil, low- and high-sulphur fuel oil), all but jet kerosene were included in Check-Run. Spot transactions by participants in these products were registered weekly with the auditors for their specified reporting area. Reporting areas were divided as follows: barge trade through Amsterdam-Rotterdam-Antwerp (the ARA) and cargo trade through the ARA ports; Hamburg-Bremen; the French Atlantic coast; and the United Kingdom east and south coasts. Of the twelve Rotterdam price series examined (which accounted for six petroleum products in barge and cargo markets), three did not generate sufficient volumes of trade to support regular, let alone daily, price reports. These were regular-grade gasoline in barges and cargoes, and naphtha in barges. Another three products (premium gasoline, low-sulphur and high-sulphur fuel oil cargoes) had sizeable markets but did not generate sufficient reports to make comparisons useful. Of those prices that could be compared, the Check-Run concluded that only three products (naphtha cargoes, gasoil cargoes, and low-sulphur fuel barges) were accurately reported.

In early 1979, the European Commission's concern about the effects that exceptionally high prices on the Rotterdam market had on worldwide oil costs led the commission to reintroduce the register of spot transactions. Comma, the second effort to register spot prices, was carried out with the purpose of understanding the structure and operation of the spot market. The results of this new exercise were more favorable to the *Platt's* price reporting procedure, indicating that there was no program that could be easily implemented to improve the present system. Specifically, the group concluded

- There is not enough justification to maintain a price reporting system on a permanent basis.
- The ability to reintroduce the register should be maintained on a standby basis. This would be accomplished in such a way that it could be quickly introduced at times of artificial disruption of the supply/demand balance.

In short, it is easier to raise objections to the reporting and the role of spot prices than it is to do something about the system. Indeed, *Platt's* has not sought the burdensome role it now holds. Rather, governments, oil companies, and traders have come to it, each seeking some independent barometer of market conditions for its own reasons. Clearly, all the users realize that *Platt's* prices should not be utilized as statistical inputs into government regulations, contract arrangements, and the like; but they justify the use of *Platt's* prices primarily by the lack of any alternative.

Introduction of Spot Price Indices

Efforts to introduce spot price indices are of more recent origin. In May 1985 the International Petroleum Exchange (IPE) of London launched a daily market index for Brent crude. This index appears at noon London time with an average price for fifteen-day cargo supplies as reported the previous day. These are spot cargoes deliverable at fifteen days' notice in the month ahead at sellers' option. The index is an average of the data from *Petroflash, Argus,* and *London Oil Reports.*

A much more extensive effort to prepare price indices (with some common features and with monitoring systems) has been launched in the growing east of Suez spot markets. A number of oil traders, refiners, and state oil refiners agreed in April 1985 to collect price data on refined products in Singapore and Japan. The price gathering effort, known as Asian Petroleum Price Index (APPI), involves seven products refined in Singapore and four products on a delivered-to-Japan basis. Participants submit price data weekly to an accountant for collating in accordance with an established formula. The resulting indices are telexed back to the paid subscribers. This industry participation scheme was developed by a trading company, Seapac Services, which is the administrator of the plan. Seapac Services appoints a panel, composed of producers, traders and refiners actively engaged in the Asian markets, which is to submit price data. Seapac also has the responsibility to keep the group "balanced."

The idea of Asian petroleum price indexing was then extended to the Asian crude markets. The Asian crude oil index monitors fourteen representative crudes, including the most important Indonesian, Malaysian, Australian, Chinese, and Middle Eastern crudes. The crude oil price index is designed to serve a necessary role of price reference in crude oil supply contracts as well as spot transactions. Some traders, however, view the market to be moving too fast to make these weekly assessments useful.

Creation of a Petroleum "Bourse"

The idea of an organized bourse (exchange) for petroleum spot trading was proposed by France in early 1979 in the hope that it could control galloping prices on the spot market and ensure that quotations were authentic and not manipulated. The feasibility of implementing the idea was then explored by the European Community (EC) in 1979–80. The proposed scenario envisaged

- Compulsory participation by all "entities" in oil trading in the EC;
- Automatic registration of all spot transactions; and
- Exclusive computer access to the "exchange" by registered entities.

The proposal was examined by a group of experts from different sectors of the oil industry, who reached the following conclusions:

- A market (in the sense of an effective trading mechanism) already exists. It differs from an official bourse in that there is no registration of membership, no official registration or reporting of transactions, no formal administrative body, and no physical trading floor. But the existence of modern telecommunication systems renders the physical centralization of trading unnecessary.
- The establishment of a formalized bourse for oil trading does not seem to be practical. Establishment of such a bourse will not significantly improve the way in which spot trade is handled.
- The initiative of the London Commodity Exchange in establishing a market in oil product futures should be recalled and followed carefully.

Introduction of Futures Markets

This chapter thus far has reviewed the way spot prices are assessed, the transparency and accuracy problems of these prices, and the efforts of governments to develop alternatives. It has been shown that, while the industry and government authorities feel substantial discomfort with these prices, most efforts to develop alternatives have ended in disappointment. It is somewhat unfortunate that the petroleum industry had to repeat the unsuccessful experiences of similar efforts in many other commodity markets just to find out that they did not work. It is fortunate, however, that the experience from other commodity markets also provides some clear guidance about what arrangements would work.

Spot trading is, in the true meaning of the word, a free-market phenomenon. Its information needs cannot be met by any controlled or even monitored arrangement. When the information need becomes strong enough, it will, through the market mechanism, develop its own answer; and the "natural" answer to a need for price transparency is the futures market. Inception of a futures market should not be undertaken by public authorities. It is simply a matter of demand and supply for price information. When there is enough demand, the market will prompt a profitability signal and entrepreneurs will respond by creating a futures exchange.

Trading in futures markets takes place on a physical floor, with deals struck by the method of open outcry. Thus, the situation is quite different from the workings of spot and term business. Open outcry means that those allowed to trade on the floor of the market face each other in a ring, and bids and offers are shouted aloud until a match is made. All participants are thus aware of every business opportunity. This information is made fully available to interested parties outside the market via visual display unit systems and is systematically reported by the financial and trade media.

The suitability of futures prices to take the leading role in price referencing is evidenced by the rapid penetration of NYMEX and IPE oil futures prices in petroleum trading decisions in the United States and Europe, respectively. Indeed, NYMEX prices have practically taken over, for the crude and products traded on this exchange, the function of price referencing in the United States. Spot prices nowadays simply follow the futures market. Most people acknowledge in New York, Houston, and, increasingly in other parts of the United States that there is little spot market trading that takes place until NYMEX actually opens in the morning.

In addition to the price-referencing function in spot trading, futures prices are increasingly used to set contract or posted prices. For example, Exxon used to adjust its heating oil postings in New York Harbor once a week, late on Friday afternoons. Now it changes postings almost daily, using the NYMEX heating oil futures price as a reference point. Another example is Conoco's use of futures prices as a component in its formula to establish posted prices.

There are three serious limitations to the usefulness of the existing futures market as a source of reference prices that would be valid worldwide:

- Problem of location—NYMEX contracts represent only one segment of the market, a specific U.S. grade delivered in a specific U.S. location. This limits the usefulness of NYMEX contracts to tra.'ers in Europe or the Far East. The International Petroleum Exchange of London and the Singapore International Monetary Exchange (SIMEX) trade petroleum futures but have not yet developed into a generally accepted source of information.

- Problem of products—NYMEX product contracts are only for regular gasoline (leaded and unleaded) and heating oil, and there is no reference price for other products. This is especially a problem with heavy fuel oil, the price of which does not seem to correlate with the products traded on NYMEX.
- Problem of quality and grades—NYMEX contracts are for specific grades of crude oil and petroleum products. Thus NYMEX prices cannot be readily used as references for other grades and qualities. This is, however, not as severe a problem as the first two. Oil traders have developed rules of thumb to arrive at some price differentials, which are used as "quality basis" to convert NYMEX prices into prices of other crudes and product qualities.

EMERGENCE OF NEW MARKER CRUDES

In the past, Saudi or Arab Light crude was the marker crude against which values of lower or higher quality oils could be set. This concept was developed in the mid-1970s when Arab Light crude emerged as the price leader on the strength of its high volume and its similarity to other OPEC crudes inside and outside the Persian Gulf. Although Saudi Light is still OPEC's de facto marker crude, it is no longer viewed in the industry as a "free" crude, and its price movements do not carry as much prominence as in the past. Instead, West Texas Intermediate (WTI) of the United States, the United Kingdom's Brent Blend, and Dubai's Fateh crude have become the new commercial marker crudes because their prices reflect market conditions more realistically.

The problem with Arab Light is that its spot price does not follow market patterns very closely. Further, the perception today is that Arab Light is not spot traded in any significant volume, and the spot price quoted is nothing more than the repetition of previous prices. While production of Arab Light is still higher than that of U.K. Brent, spot trading of Arab Light is very small. In addition, WTI and Brent are extensively traded on the futures and forward markets.

WTI is becoming central to world oil market prices. Highly visible price quotes on NYMEX account for much of this phenomenon. Technically, WTI is an unlikely world market indicator, since physical supplies are largely landlocked in the U.S. midcontinent pipeline system and are nonexportable. WTI prices reflect U.S. buyer thinking but often do not match precisely with landed prices of imported crudes due to differences in trading practices. For example, WTI trades in minimum parcels of 10,000 to 50,000 barrels a month, with a few deals in the range of 150,000 to 300,000 barrels a month. This compares with typical world market crude cargoes of 600,000 to 1.8 million barrels.

The central delivery location for WTI is in Cushing, Oklahoma, where several large pipelines with about 1 million b/d capacity converge. Some supplies are also routinely exchanged for similar domestic oils further south, near the big Texas coastal refining centers. WTI is gathered over a wide area, both by truck and small pipelines, converging in the Midland, Texas area, where it is either routed north to Cushing (hence to the inland Chicago and upper midwestern refineries) or to the Texas refineries. In addition to Texas crudes, Cushing is a center for the Oklahoma gathering system, which has 20 million barrels of storage capacity.

Brent's elevation to the status of marker crude is primarily due to the substantial sales of this crude in the physical market and, more importantly, to enormous volumes of speculative trading on the forward market.[8] In addition, the recent move to abolish the state oil trading company, British National Oil Corporation (BNOC), has further exposed the Brent to market fluctuations. The Brent spot price is now widely monitored and is often used as a yardstick by other producers, especially those in West Africa and the Mediterranean. The emphasis on Brent trading is, however, shifting towards hedging—with traders and refiners buying or selling forward increasing volumes of Brent to cover their future sales or purchases of Mideast, African, and even other North Sea grades. The forward Brent market provides an effective hedging tool because of its liquidity and price quotes up to six months forward. European refiners often prefer this forward market to the futures market because they can cover large quantities without making waves on the market. Also, because of its large-sized deals and unstable prices, the Brent spot market is becoming concentrated in the hands of a few major traders, including the integrated oil companies, large New York investment banks, and Japanese trading houses.

Dubai's Fateh crude—sometimes called the "Brent of the East"—has now turned into the primary spot crude of the Persian Gulf. Also, forward sales have become an established element of the market for this crude. Fateh is viewed as a free crude because

- Its output is free of OPEC limits;
- Its production (350,000 b/d) is sold by several firms rather than a single company; and

- Its quality is similar to Arab Light.

The market for Fateh crude, however, differs from that of Brent in that

- Forward trading is confined to one or two months ahead, as compared with Brent's four to six months;
- Most participants intend to obtain physical delivery and do not move in and out of paper barrel positions as with North Sea oil; and
- Price differentials on forward months tend to be smaller than those in the Brent market.

Finally, in the Mediterranean, Libya's lighter Es Sider grade is developing into something of a regional reference crude due primarily to barter deals and the diversity of its suppliers. Forward deals are limited to two months, often resulting from barter volumes sold in advance, rather than speculative interest. In spite of its significant output of about 400,000 b/d, the influence of Es Sider is kept fairly local since it cannot by U.S. law move to the large U.S. market where, at present, light sweet crudes enjoy premium values.

PART THREE

Futures Market

Petroleum futures markets have, in the last decade, grown very rapidly, with a profound impact on spot trading. It has now become a common practice in the United States not to transact a spot trade before considering the NYMEX futures prices.

Petroleum futures were, until the early 1980s, dismissed by many industry analysts as of no significance in the oil business. Today, most people accept that petroleum futures are here to stay, but there is still controversy over how important a role futures will play. Some analysts view oil futures as a "paper market" with no significant relationship to the real market. Others argue that oil futures have changed the structure of the petroleum market considerably. This controversy is due partly to differences of opinion on the structure of the petroleum market and partly to widespread confusion about the workings of the futures market and the manner in which it interacts with the spot market. Part Three describes the mechanism of futures trading and the means by which it interacts with the spot market.

CHAPTER 5

The Mechanics of Futures Trading

HOW FUTURES TRADING WORKS

An example of how futures trading works is described below. The example is based on the assumption that a distributor is holding 100,000 barrels of heating oil for delivery to his customers in December. He is committed to supplying the heating oil at the spot market price at the time of delivery. The petroleum market is unstable and he fears that the price of petroleum products (including heating oil) may decline substantially by the time of delivery. A change in the price of heating oil from $0.60 per gallon to $0.55 per gallon would leave him with a loss of $210,000. Thus, a decision to hold on to his inventory would be very risky. A clear alternative is to sell the inventory on the spot market and reacquire it before the month in which he has a delivery commitment.

A much more convenient alternative by which the distributor could keep his stock of heating oil, thus avoiding the price risk, is to sign a contract with an "agent" to whom the distributor sells the 100,000 barrels of heating oil at a set price (say $0.60) for delivery in December. In this way, the price risk is transferred to that agent and the distributor will bear no loss if the price drops by December. He has sold his heating oil inventory at the price of $0.60 a gallon, and he will receive this price regardless of the spot price in December. All of the loss will be borne by the buying agent. Of course, in such a risky market situation, everything may work the other way around. The price of heating oil may jump to $0.70 a gallon. The distributor would have earned $420,000 in capital gains if he had not signed the contract. But since he has signed the contract, the buying agent receives the gain. In sum, the buying agent accepts the risk and, therefore, receives all the possible gains and losses associated with risk.

What happens in December? The distributor needs the heating oil for delivery to his own customers, but, at the same time, he has an obligation to deliver the heating oil to the buying agent. This is where the futures market mechanism solves the problem. The buying agent has the option of selling his contract to the initial seller (the hypothetical distributor above) or to any other agent. Thus, by the time the contract is due, the distributor buys back the contract (of course, at a different price).

The futures market mechanism provides two important facilities for this distributor. First, by December when the distributor wants to buy back his contract, the futures market (almost) guarantees that he can purchase the contract and avoid the actual delivery of the heating oil to the buying agent. This is due to the fact that the contract itself will have its own market along with its own demand and supply forces. The contract will then always be available to buy or to sell at the appropriate price. Second, the distributor's possible loss or gain from selling and buying back the contract is (normally) offset by his gain or loss on the value of his inventory due to the change in the spot market price. In this way he protects himself from market risk.

MARKET PARTICIPANTS

The aforementioned distributor intended to protect himself from the risk associated with a change in the price of heating oil. In this sense, he is normally called a "hedger." In order to find someone who is willing to take over the risk of the price change, the distributor goes to a *futures exchange*. A *futures exchange* is nothing more than a central meeting place for buyers and sellers (or their representatives) to transact business. They enter into special contracts for the future delivery of commodities: these contracts are known as *futures*. Each contract specifies the exact quality of the commodity, the month of delivery, and the place (or places) at which delivery is to be made. A futures contract is a promise on behalf of the seller to deliver within a specified month and a promise on behalf of the buyer to take delivery of a standard quality and quantity of the commodity at an agreed price. In most futures markets, however, only a small fraction of contracts sold is closed by delivery of the commodity. Since nearly all participants are motivated by the desire to trade on price movements, they liquidate by undertaking offsetting transactions. The buyer can liquidate his position in the futures market prior to delivery of the commodity by selling contracts of the same futures. For each contract purchased or sold and subsequently liquidated, the trader takes a total profit or loss equal to the difference between his buying and selling price multiplied by the number of units of the commodity specified in the contract.

Three groups of people are involved in the futures market. First, there is a *selling hedger*. A selling hedger is a producer, or a stockholder, who possesses (or will possess) the commodity and wants to protect himself against a fall in its price; he will sell a futures contract to hedge against a price fall. Second, there is a *buying hedger*. The buying hedger is, again, a user or stockpiler of a commodity. He will need the commodity for some time in the future; he does not intend to buy it now. He buys a futures contract to hedge against a possible price rise. And third, there is the speculator. He participates in both buying and selling of futures. He is neither a producer nor a stockholder nor a user of the commodity. This individual enters the market with only one goal in mind—to make a profit from correctly anticipating the direction of prices. By assuming the risk that the producers and processors desire to avoid, the speculator stands to lose money if his judgment proves wrong.

Selling Hedger

A selling hedger, a person in the first group described above, will take a "short position" in the futures market and a "long position" in the actual (spot) market. For example, a jobber who is going to have 100,000 barrels of product in his inventory next month is called "long in the actual market." The hedging action would require him to sell a 100,000-barrel futures contract for delivery the next month. He will be short in the futures market.

If the spot market price (also known as the cash market price) of petroleum products is currently $23.00/b, the jobber's position in the market is worth $2,300,000 because he is holding 100,000 barrels. His position in the futures market is also worth $2,300,000 because he has sold 100,000 barrels of the next month's delivery at the price of $23.00/b

Exhibit 5.1
A Hedge

Status

A distributor is holding 100,000 barrels of heating oil to deliver to his customers in December.

Concern

He is concerned that petroleum prices may fall by December and he may lose on the value of his inventory.

Hedging Action

(1) He signs a contract with an "agent" and sells 100,000 barrels of heating oil for delivery in December at the present market price.

(2) He buys back (liquidates) the above contract in November at the then current price.

Results

(1) He loses, or gains, in the value of his inventory in proportion to the fall, or rise, in the price.

(2) He gains, or loses, in the value of his contract with that agent in proportion to the fall, or rise, in the price.

(3) His loss, or gain, in item 1 under Results is offset by his gain, or loss, in item 2 under Results.

Futures market provides the distributor with

(1) A place to find that buying "agent."

(2) The possibility to buy back his contract in November.

If, however, by the next month, the spot market price drops to $21.00/b, the jobber's position will then deteriorate from $2,300,000 to $2,100,000; that is, he will have a $200,000 capital loss in the spot market. At the same time, however, he buys back his futures contract. The spot price will have declined by $2.00/b, the futures prices have declined by almost the same amount. Consequently, he will buy back the futures contract at $21.00/b. Since he had sold this contract at $23.00, and is now buying it back at $21.00, the gain on futures trading ($2.00 x 100,000 = $200,000) offsets the loss in the spot market. This situation is normally known as a "perfect" or "efficient" hedge. In practice, however, the spot market price and the futures price may not move in such a parallel fashion; therefore, the gain and loss to the hedger may not completely offset each other.

Buying Hedger

A buying hedger, a person in the second group, will take a short position in the spot market and a long position in the futures market. For example, a refiner decides he needs 200,000 barrels of crude next November. He does not need to buy the crude now. However, he fears that by next November the price of crude may have increased. To avoid the price risk, the refiner buys 200 November contracts (each contract is for 1,000 barrels). If prices happen to go up during this period, he will not be affected by the price increase because he has already made the deal at the specific price; if, on the other hand, prices decline, the refiner will not be able to gain from the price decrease because he has obligated himself to buy the crude at the agreed price.

It is, however, important to note that a buying hedger (the refiner, for example) does not normally use the futures market as a source of supply. It is true that the refiner can plan on taking delivery; in such a case, the seller of the contract is obligated to make the delivery. The usual practice is, however, to close the futures contract before its maturity date. That is, futures transactions do not really require the physical delivery or even physical existence of the oil being traded. Participants simply sell an "obligation to take or make delivery" and buy back this obligation before it reaches maturity. Thus, the refiner buys his crude on the spot market at the same time that he sells his futures contract. His gain or loss on a futures contract will compensate for the change in the spot value of the crude so that he is not affected by any price movement occurring between the present and next November. He is still using the spot market as the source of supply but he utilizes the futures market to protect himself against price variations.

Speculators

A speculator, a person in the third group, will sell a futures contract when he expects the prices to fall. He may sell oil futures to a refiner who will need the crude in two months. The speculator does not own the oil he contracts to deliver; nor does he want to own that oil. His only aim is to profit on a downward price movement. Thus, if the price does indeed fall between the time he sells the oil futures and the time he must deliver it, he will make a profit. He can then enter the market and buy back his contract at a profit without even having seen a barrel of oil. Conversely, the speculator will lose money if his judgment proves wrong and he must purchase the oil futures contract at a price higher than the price at which he initially sold the contract. In the same way, a speculator will buy oil futures if he anticipates a price rise. Again, he will sell his futures before maturity (the delivery month) and will make a profit if the price has increased.

WHY SOME PEOPLE HEDGE AND SOME SPECULATE

In early discussions and writings on futures trading, the hedger was often described as an apparently "unsophisticated" participant in futures trading who regards the making of prices as a full-time occupation for "experts." Speculators, on the other hand, were viewed as "professional dealers" who study the market systematically and have access to more information. Thus, the speculator receives a premium for his higher level of "wisdom" and "sophistication."

A somewhat more classical explanation for the speculator's role in the futures market is that people are naturally different: some avoid risk and others take it. The discussion in the literature about the behavior of so-called risk-averse people versus risk lovers and risk-neutral individuals is very involved and theoretical. And, despite its intellectual appeal, it has not yet provided much explanation for practical issues concerning the futures market. In particular, theory on the role of speculators offers little explanation as to why a company (whose decision makers may presumably consist of risk averters as well as risk lovers) should consistently act as a speculator or as a hedger.

A more recent explanation for futures trading is that both sellers and buyers of any futures contract base their decisions on speculation. However, two different types of information are available to them, which may result in two different types of speculation. In this respect, the futures market is assumed to provide a means of sharing information. This information may come from several sources. First, speculators may have studied market conditions and acquired information that is not readily available to others. Second, each speculator may specialize in a certain part of the market (e.g., demand for oil by sector or region, or supply by each group of producers): his participation in futures trading will move the price towards the direction indicated by this special information. Third, the futures market provides a means of pooling all the information that individual suppliers and consumers may have about conditions in the futures market.

According to the above theory, speculation takes place based on the endowment of information. Agents or individuals who have access to more accurate information receive more profit from their engagement in futures trading. Therefore, these agents or individuals sell their information (or at least part of it) and the speculative gain they acquire is the price for this information.

Holbrook Working, a prominent leader in the field, and his followers have introduced a new theory regarding speculation and hedging in futures markets. According to their line of reasoning, the hedger does not primarily seek to avoid risk. Rather, he hedges because of an expected return arising from anticipation of favorable relative price movements in the spot and futures markets. It is not realistic to view the trader purely as a hedger or a speculator. Each trader chooses a combination of hedging and speculation as a form of "arbitrage." This line of reasoning is probably one of the first attempts to analyze the fundamentals of futures trading within the framework of conventional theories of economics.

Mr. Working views both hedging and speculation as multipurpose trade decisions that are, at any time, aimed at various goals. On the hedging side, he names five different types:

- Carrying-charge hedging;
- Operational hedging;
- Selective hedging;
- Anticipatory hedging;
- Pure risk-avoidance hedging.

Carrying-charge hedging is done simultaneously with the holding of the commodity stock for direct profit from storage. Operational hedging is done to facilitate operations involved in the merchandising or "processing business." Selective hedging, which is based on price expectations, refers to incomplete hedging but is used by producers and processors as a substitute for a merchandising contract. Finally, pure risk-avoidance hedging may be what people have in mind when they talk about hedging. Mr. Working's main argument is that pure risk-avoidance hedging is almost nonexistent in the real world. That is, hedging is (almost) always aimed at several objectives, one of which may be risk avoidance.

With regard to the other side of trading, Mr. Working classifies the role of speculation in futures markets into four categories:

- Price-level trading (or position trading);
- News trading;
- Scalping;
- Trend trading.

Price-level trading refers to speculation based on the economics of the market. The speculator uses his information about the demand and supply of the commodity to judge whether the current price is higher than, lower than, or equal to the level warranted by market conditions. News trading refers to the type of speculation that is based on early access to news about the demand and supply of a commodity. The trader makes his move based on such news and then publicizes the value of that news in determining market movements. Scalping is buying on price dips and selling on price bulges. These dips and bulges normally arise from speculative buying or selling, and last for a very short period of time (a few minutes to a few days). Finally, trend trading refers to profit speculations from "riding" the price trend. Again, Mr. Working's argument is that speculative trading is always a combination of several types of trading, and one cannot limit the explanation of speculative trading to only one of these types.

INVESTMENT OPPORTUNITIES

Traditionally, the return on investment in futures trading has been known to include a risk premium. Hedgers wish to avoid the risk of any price movement. Speculators provide the hedgers with a price-insurance service. They are paid for this service in the form of an insurance premium that materializes as a discount on the futures prices relative to the spot market price that is expected to prevail at the maturity date of the futures contract. Thus, investment in futures trading is somewhat riskier than investment in, say, stocks and bonds. However, the risk involved in futures trading is related primarily to the mechanism of futures trading.

Investment in a futures market differs in an important way from most other investments. An investor in stocks and bonds, for example, has to pay the total amount of his investment at the time he is making this investment. Clearly, he can borrow part of the funds, but essentially there is no difference in the opportunity cost of his investment. Commodity contracts, on the other hand, present the investor with a different situation. The contract is an agreement between a seller and a buyer for the delivery of a commodity at a specified date for a specific price. The initial investment on this agreement is a relatively small deposit to assure the financial ability of the buyer and seller. This deposit, called the margin, is about 3–5 percent for most commodity tradings, but for petroleum futures, the margin has been increased to about 20 percent of the contract value to safeguard against drastic volatility of petroleum prices. However, the gains and losses of the contract to the investor are based on the total value of the contract. For example, if an investor buys a contract of 1,000 barrels (42,000 U.S. gallons) of heating oil at a price of $0.60 per gallon, the value of the contract will be: $0.60 x 42,000 = $25,200. The margin he deposits is only about $5,000. If the price of heating oil increases by 10 percent, his profit will be $2,520. If this profit is compared with the initial money he invested ($5,000), the rate of return will be about 50 percent. In the same manner, a 10 percent decline in the price of heating oil will result in a loss of about 50 percent. Thus, investment in futures trading involves a high (positive or negative) rate of return only when profits or losses are compared with the deposited margin.

The above explanation of the investment mechanism in futures trading indicates that this investment should, in general, be much riskier than investment in stocks and bonds. However, empirical research has shown that while the average return on futures trading is about the same as that on common stock, the variation of the rate of return in futures trading is less than that for common stock, given a diversified portfolio of commodity futures. That is, investment in futures trading is, on average, less risky than investment in common stocks. Furthermore, the rate of return on futures trading is substantially higher than the return on common stocks during inflationary periods: futures trading provides a better hedge against inflation than does investment in common stocks. During years of low inflation, however, common stocks yield a higher rate of return. All of the evidence suggests that an investor who keeps a portfolio of stocks and bonds may be substantially better off to include some holdings of futures contracts in his portfolio. This suggestion has been empirically supported only when the investor holds a diversified combination of commodity futures.

In short, investment opportunities in futures trading are not homogeneous to all traders. Empirical research has shown that hedgers do

Exhibit 5.2
Losers and Winners of the Game

Hedgers
• They buy price insurance at a low premium.

Small speculators
• They are the net losers of the game.

Large speculators
• They maintain more comprehensive and updated information about the market.
• They have the financial ability to stay in the market for a longer period of time.
• They are the net winners of the game.

---

not pay much "insurance premium" and thus, there is no guaranteed minimum return to be gained by all speculators. Rather, speculators win from each other. Large speculators usually make a consistent profit, whereas small speculators are, on average, the net losers of the trade. To be a winner, one has to be a better speculator than others.

CHAPTER 6

Evolution of Futures Markets

FROM FORWARD CONTRACTS TO FUTURES TRADING

Futures markets have evolved from the so-called forward trading, which dates back at least to the seventeenth century. A forward contract is an agreement for the sale (or purchase) of a commodity at a specified time in the future at a certain price. It differs from a futures contract mainly in that the forward contract is not standardized with respect to quantity, quality, and location of trade. Rather, each contract is tailored to the special needs of a specific seller and buyer.

The formal emergence of futures markets occurred in the nineteenth century when futures trading started in the United States, the United Kingdom, Germany, and elsewhere. The oldest commodity exchange in the United States is the Chicago Board of Trade (CBT), which was founded in 1848 and began futures trading in 1865. Other exchanges began their trading in the second half of the nineteenth century.

Futures markets currently exist for a wide array of real and financial assets, including grains and feeds, livestock, industrial raw materials, precious metals, financial instruments, and foreign currencies. In particular, the last two decades have witnessed a dramatic increase in the types of contracts traded, and in the volume of transactions and open interest. In the United States, the volume of transactions in futures increased from less than 4 million contracts in 1960 to over 230 million in 1990. The average open interest increased from about 140,000 contracts in 1960 to about 4 million in 1990. Many European countries have also observed expanding futures markets. London exchanges are actively involved in futures trading of cocoa, coffee, copper, cotton, grains, rubber, and metals. The Bourse de Commerce of Paris and the Stitching Cocatermijn market in Amsterdam have turned into important futures markets. In Asia, there are numerous commodity exchanges in Japan, India, Malaysia, and Singapore. The most important exchange in Japan is the Tokyo Grain and Commodity Exchange. In India, there are a number of exchanges that trade cotton, groundnuts, etc., while in Malaysia there are futures markets in rubber. Singapore offers futures in petroleum. What are the main factors behind the development of futures markets? Why have the futures trading of some commodities expanded so vastly while many other commodities have never been subject to futures trading or have failed to become futures commodities after being introduced on one or several exchanges in the United States or other countries? A futures market typically develops in response to economic forces in the spot market. If the characteristics of the spot market are suitable, a futures market will emerge. After its development, the futures market will facilitate the operation of the spot market. Thus, futures markets are not invented or imposed on the spot market, but, rather, they evolve out of the need to have functions performed that the existing marketing system is not performing effectively.

Futures trading was introduced in response to seasonal fluctuations in the supply of crops. In particular, many authors refer to the corn trade in Chicago as an important step in the emergence of forward and futures contracts. In fact, a review of the Chicago corn trade is a useful exercise in understanding the prospect for futures trading in other commodities. After the opening of the Illinois-Michigan canal, substantial corn trading began along the river. Farmers produced corn and hauled it to local elevators. Merchants built corn cribs for subsequent shipment to Chicago.

Farmers hauled corn during the late autumn and winter when the roads and/or canals were frozen. The merchants stored the corn until spring and then shipped it to Chicago. The merchants, of course, had to make a relatively large capital investment to build and maintain the inventory. At the same time, however, farmers wanted payment on delivery of the corn to the merchants. Merchants, then, needed considerable liquidity while they carried the risk of a decline in price until spring when they would ship and sell the corn in Chicago. The merchants could not get much help from the bankers: because of the great price risk involved in holding corn from autumn to spring, bankers were reluctant to make large loans on the unsold corn. Thus, the price risk was a barrier to the efficient operation of the market by all agents involved in the market: farmers, merchants, financial institutions, and consumers.

A logical extension of the market was the development of forward contracts. The merchants would go to Chicago and make a contract, at a firm price, for the delivery of corn in the spring. This forward contract solved many of the problems in the market: bankers viewed the forward contract as a desirable collateral for issuing loans; merchants were free of price risk and behaved more rationally while dealing with farmers; and farmers found market conditions more suitable, which added to the efficiency of their operation.

Forward contracting, which then became a common practice in trading other agricultural crops, was initially limited to individuals who were somehow involved in the production, storage, processing, or consumption of these commodities. However, as time passed, four new dimensions were incorporated into these contracts, which finally led to the formal introduction of futures trading. First, for the purpose of promoting the commerce of Chicago, the city's Board of Trade was designated as the official agency for the measurement, weighing, and inspection of grains. This led to the development of quality standards that, in turn, facilitated the trade even for those who did not know much about grains. Second, an organized exchange (Chicago Board of Trade) was introduced as the marketplace for those who wanted to buy or sell forward contracts. Third, contracts became increasingly transferable, allowing a buyer of a contract to sell his contract before the time of delivery. Fourth, the trading of forward contracts was expanded to cover a new group of people—speculators—who were not actually involved in the production, storage, processing, or consumption of the commodity but who viewed the forward contract deals as "a paper market," which was very suitable for making a fast profit.

In this manner, forward contracting developed into futures trading. The administration of futures trading, however, has gone through many ups and downs since its inception. Numerous modifications have been made to the rules of trade and the organization of various exchanges. More importantly, the attitude of legislators and public authorities with regard to the nature and legitimacy of futures trading has changed significantly. In 1867, the Illinois state legislature passed a bill that declared all futures contracts a form of gambling and thus void, except for cases in which the seller was the owner or agent for the owner of the grain at the time the contract was made. Similarly, many other public authorities objected to futures trading, perceiving it as an instrument speculators could use to manipulate the spot market. Speculators, on the other hand, had found futures trading an exciting game that held out the promise of huge profits. They rushed into the futures markets and took the play away from commercial traders. Public concern grew over price distortions and even the "immorality" of futures trading. Consequently, futures trading became subject to increasing government influence and control.

At present, futures trading is a closely regulated activity. The purpose of existing regulations is to maintain the competitiveness and fairness of trade. To this end, the regulatory body of each country attempts, in one way or another, to govern the relationship of an exchange with its members and that of the members with each other. The appropriate level of government intervention is still a subject of controversy. However, futures trading is now a publicly accepted activity and is viewed as an example of a competitive market.

In the United States, futures markets were first regulated by the federal government in 1921. In the early 1930s, futures trading turned into a legislative issue, with the U.S. Congress passing the Commodity Exchange Act, which assigned to the Department of Agriculture the responsibility of monitoring the activities of futures trading (this was due to the fact that futures trading was then limited to agricultural commodities). After the significant increase in the level of futures trading in the early 1970s, the U.S. Congress decided to establish an independent federal agency to pursue the task. To this end, the Commodity Futures Trading Commission (CFTC) was created in 1974. The CFTC has been chartered by Congress to license futures exchanges, to approve the terms and conditions of any futures contract before it is introduced on an exchange, and to monitor the implementation of commodity regulations on all U.S. exchanges. The CFTC is especially responsible for detecting and investigating problems involving market manipulation.

FUTURES TRADING IN THE PETROLEUM MARKET

Although futures trading in the petroleum market is a recent phenomenon, forward trading has existed in this market for a long time. Contract sales with fixed (or predictably fixed) prices have served the industry as a form of forward trade for several decades. At present, however, revisions, discounts, and premiums to the posted price are becoming the rule rather than the exception. Furthermore, many contract prices are now related to the spot market price. Thus, contract sales have lost their forward-trading characteristics, creating an opportunity for futures trading to provide price insurance to petroleum traders.

Petroleum futures developed in response to instability in petroleum prices. "First-generation" petroleum futures, which were introduced in 1974, came about as a reaction to the 1973–74 fluctuations in the price of oil. These futures failed for various reasons, the most important of which was the relatively stable price that prevailed in the market in 1975. "Second-generation" petroleum futures started with the introduction of a heating oil contract in 1978; it then expanded to include several futures in crude oil and petroleum products.

First-generation futures trading in the petroleum market began with the introduction of a crude oil contract on the New York Cotton Exchange in autumn 1974. The contract called for the delivery of crude at Rotterdam. Technical specifications of the contract (34 °API and 1.7 percent sulphur content) matched those of Saudi light crude. However, the contract provided the seller with an option to deliver other qualities (varying from 27–45 °API and 0.1–0.3 percent sulphur content) of crude at a discount or premium. In the same year, NYMEX introduced two contracts—a Bunker C futures and a gasoil futures—both of which required delivery at Rotterdam.

All of the first-generation contracts failed to attract the petroleum industry and faded into obscurity. There were several reasons for this failure, the most important of which was that petroleum prices did not fluctuate as expected. The international spot price of crude oil stayed between $10.30 and $10.46 a barrel during the period of October 1974 to December 1975. Price stability was further reinforced in the United States when the U.S. Congress passed the Energy Policy and Conservation Act in 1975. The act limited the annual increase of the price of crude oil, which led to reasonable predictability of petroleum prices.

The second reason for the failure of these futures was the petroleum industry's lack of participation in trading these futures. The presumption that the petroleum futures market, like that of other commodities, can expand without the participation of the petroleum industry proved to be wrong. The industry's lack of participation was, in turn, related to two discouraging factors. First, the requirement for Rotterdam delivery was a technical inconvenience for U.S. refiners, jobbers, distributors, and consumers. Although the oil industry had been told that futures contracts provided financial protection and that there was no reason to worry about delivery, the industry could not see the rationale of buying or selling a contract that specified a delivery point so far away from the domestic market. Second, futures markets were unknown to the oil industry, and there were serious concerns about their impact on the petroleum business.

Second-generation futures began with the introduction of two contracts on NYMEX in November 1978. The first contract called for the delivery of No. 2 heating oil with a gravity of 30 °API and a maximum sulphur content of 0.2 percent. The second contract called for the delivery of No. 6 fuel oil with a gravity of 10–30 °API and a maximum sulphur content of 0.3 percent. Both contracts were for delivery of 42,000 U.S. gallons (1,000 barrels) in the New York Harbor area. (The provisions of these contracts, as well as other petroleum futures, are discussed later.)

The No. 2 heating oil turned into a successful energy future after a few months of slow trading. Its trade volume reached 34 million barrels in 1979, followed by 238 million, 995 million, and 1.754 billion barrels in 1980, 1981, and 1982, respectively. The volume of trade reached 25 million b/d in 1990. The success of this future was due to several factors. First, gasoil was exempted from price controls in more than forty states in 1976. Second, the international price of oil has been very volatile since late 1978. Third, the complete deregulation of U.S. oil prices by the Reagan administration in February 1981 forged a stronger link between domestic prices and volatile international prices. Fourth, NYMEX has consistently attempted to communicate the uses of its futures contracts to the petroleum industry.

The success of the heating oil contract encouraged NYMEX and other exchanges to introduce other petroleum futures. In August 1981, NYMEX introduced another heating oil contract that specified delivery in the Gulf Coast area. This contract became dormant because traders were presumably more comfortable trading in the already established New York heating oil market. The volume of trade for the Gulf Coast heating oil reached around 1.8 million barrels in 1981 and ceased in 1982.

In October 1981, NYMEX introduced a contract for unleaded gasoline. The delivery location for this contract was New York Harbor and the unit of trade was 42,000 U.S. gallons. This contract only recently became very successful. Its volume of trade reached about 22 million b/d in 1990.

Probably the most important event in the energy futures market was the introduction on March 30, 1983, of a crude oil futures contract at

NYMEX. This contract called for the delivery of 1,000 barrels of sweet crude at Cushing Storage, Oklahoma. The par crude was West Texas Intermediate with 40 °API and 0.4 percent sulphur content. Other types of crude (U.K. Brent Blend, Nigerian Brass Blend and Bonny Light, Norwegian Ekofisk, Tunisian Zarzaitine, Algerian Saharan Blend, Mid-Continent Sweet, New Mexican Sweet, and South Texas Sweet) were, however, all acceptable for delivery at certain premiums or discounts. Cushing was chosen as the delivery point because it is common for companies to trade crude oil there. Fourteen crude oil pipelines now flow in and out of Cushing and an average of 35 million barrels of oil flows through Cushing each month. Crude oil futures began with an average daily volume of 700,000 barrels. Its total volume of trade during 1983 was 323 million barrels, and its average daily volume reached 5 million barrels in 1984. In 1990, trading volume reached 100 million b/d.

Benefiting from NYMEX's experience, a petroleum futures market was established in London. This market, called the International Petroleum Exchange (IPE), introduced its first contract in April 1981. The contract was for 100 tonnes (733 barrels) of gasoil and was priced in U.S. dollars per contract. Delivery was designated at specified tank installations in the Amsterdam, Rotterdam, and Antwerp area.

The total volume of IPE's gasoil trade in 1981 reached 14.9 million tonnes, which is equivalent to 109 million barrels. This quantity represents an average volume of trade of 670,000 b/d. In 1982, the total volume of trade soared to 454 million barrels, which indicates a daily trade volume of 1.8 million barrels. The volume of trade increased progressively, reaching about two billion barrels in 1990.

The rapid growth of IPE's gasoil futures during 1981–82 was not primarily due to the entry of new traders in the market. Rather, it was the result of an increase in the level of trade activity by those already in the market. A survey sponsored by IPE shows that about 160 companies use IPE's gasoil contract. However, more than 50 percent of the total trade is accounted for by twenty-five companies. This finding indicates that the market can still expand in two ways: first, the volume of trade can grow significantly if the many small users already in the market intensify their trade to a level comparable with that of the leaders; second, the market can expand considerably by attracting new participants. The rapid increase in trading volume during 1987–90 was, however, due to the entry of more oil companies and traders who use the futures markets both as a hedge and as a medium for buying and selling physical supplies.

Encouraged by the success of its gasoil futures, IPE introduced a crude oil contract in November 1983. Each contract specified 1,000 barrels of Brent Blend. Other crudes (Ninian Blend, Forties Blend, Ekofisk Blend, Bonny Light, Brass River, Zarzaitine, and Saharan Blend) would also be delivered at appropriate premiums or discounts. The basis for delivery was into tank, pipeline, or FOB Rotterdam/Amsterdam or by in-tank transfer in Rotterdam/Amsterdam for deliveries of less than fifty lots. In addition, the contract terms provided an alternative delivery procedure under which the buyer and seller could agree (in the month prior to Rotterdam/Amsterdam delivery becoming due) to alternative delivery terms.

Crude oil trading on IPE was not initially successful. The total volume of trade during 1983 was about 2.8 million barrels. In February 1984 the daily volume reached 77,000 barrels and then declined very sharply to negligible levels in March and April. IPE introduced a revised crude oil contract in November 1985, but it again failed to attract a sufficient number of participants. Finally, IPE introduced a new crude oil contract in June 1988 with settlement terms designed to fit with the Brent forward market. This contract was well received by the petroleum industry. Owing to this success, IPE introduced a high-sulphur fuel oil (HSFO) contract in September 1989.

Finally, the most recent addition to the petroleum futures markets was the introduction of the two petroleum contracts at the Singapore International Monetary Exchange (SIMEX) during 1989 and 1990. The first contract, which was introduced in February 1989, calls for the delivery of 100 metric tons of HSFO. The main reason for the choice of HSFO as the underlying commodity for the futures contract was the extensive use of this product in the region, particularly in the shipping industry.

The second energy futures contract, introduced in June 1990, calls for delivery of 1,000 barrels of Dubai crude oil. An important feature of this contract is that the contract does not call for the physical delivery of the oil. Instead, it will be closed by cash settlement. The final settlement price of the expiring contract will be determined by SIMEX's clearinghouse. To determine the prevailing market price for the Dubai crude oil, the clearinghouse will have to obtain price assessments from at least twenty reference firms and corporations and then compute a settlement price.

The crude oil contract at SIMEX will eventually be complemented by a similar contract at IPE to provide near round-the-clock access to Dubai futures trading. The IPE contract also calls for delivery of 1,000 barrels and is based on a cash settlement rather than physical delivery. These contract characteristics have been designed so that the two exchanges can formally link together and trade the same contract worldwide twenty-four hours a day.

Unlike the significant success of NYMEX and IPE with petroleum futures, the Chicago Board of Trade (CBT) experienced consistent failure with several petroleum futures contracts. CBT introduced petroleum futures in unleaded gasoline, No. 2 heating oil, and crude oil. The unleaded gasoline futures commenced trading in December 1982. Each contract called for the delivery of 1,000 barrels of regular unleaded gasoline, standard Colonial Pipeline specifications, and a southern grade with a minimum of 87.0 and a maximum of less than 91.0 octane rating. The delivery location was the Texas Gulf Coast, but the mechanism of delivery was the so-called depository-receipt method. This method required that the seller of the contract obtain a depository receipt from an issuer approved by the exchange. The volume of trade of unleaded gasoline on CBT was about 8.7 million barrels in 1982, which represented an average daily volume of about 600,000 barrels. In early 1983, the volume increased to an average of 800,000 b/d. Since April 1983, however, it began to decline and went dormant by the end of the year. The main reason for the failure of the contract seems to be its delivery method. Oil traders prefer a wet-barrel delivery over the depository-receipt system.

In March 1983, CBT introduced a crude oil contract on the same day that NYMEX opened its crude oil futures. CBT's contract called for 1,000 barrels of Light Louisiana Sweet, while other crudes (Bonny Light, Brass River, Ekofisk, Qua Iboi, Saharan Blend, and Zarzaitine) would be deliverable at appropriate premiums or discounts. The delivery location was the Capline System in St. James, Louisiana, or other seller-designated port facilities in St. James, St. John the Baptist, St. Charles, Jefferson, Orleans, St. Bernard, or Plaquemines parishes, Louisiana. The delivery method was in wet barrels. CBT's crude oil contract initially performed better than the gasoline contract but eventually failed. Its total volume of trade in 1983 reached 93 million barrels, which represented an average daily volume of about 400,000 barrels. But the volume of trade declined over time and practically halted by the end of 1984. Trade analysts believe that the depository-receipt delivery method of unleaded gasoline and No. 2 heating oil had a negative impact on the desirability of CBT's crude oil contract. Traders hesitated to

Table 6.1
Participants in NYMEX's Energy Futures in 1987 (number of companies)

	Crude oil futures	Heavy oil futures	Unleaded gasoline futures
Integrated oil companies	12	11	12
Refiners	8	4	9
Producers	4	—	—
Trader-resellers	7	14	12
Traders	17	16	22
End user	—	—	—
Total number of participants	48	46	56

take a simultaneous position in crude and product futures when the crude futures called for delivery in wet barrels and the product futures stipulated depository receipts. Further, the designated premiums for foreign crude discouraged the trade.

Finally, CBT introduced a No. 2 heating oil contract in April 1983. This contract called for the delivery of 1,000 barrels of heating oil in Harris, Galveston, or Jefferson counties, Texas. The delivery method was the depository-receipt mechanism. Despite the success of the heating oil contracts at NYMEX and IPE, CBT's heating oil contract did not experience high volumes of trade and died a few months later.

OIL INDUSTRY PARTICIPATION

Despite initial resistance to the development of petroleum futures, the petroleum industry has taken an active role in futures and options trading (see Table 6.1). A survey carried out in 1987 indicates the integrated oil companies account for about 21 percent of traders at NYMEX. Every oil company, whether large or small, takes risks in order to be productive and profitable. Each segment of the business, from upstream exploration for crude oil to downstream refining and marketing of refined petroleum products, involves risk. Integrated oil companies must balance the total system, from crude production to product distribution, to produce the most profitable product slate. Companies strive to establish the best cost/value relationship available in each operating segment in order to maximize profit margins. This effort requires significant know-how, management skills, and operating flexibility with respect to refinery processes, market economies, and changing product inventories and demand. Because of limitations on each company's supply, refining, and distribution system, there is risk and price exposure that must be managed. A continual process of pricing, buying, selling, trading, and scheduling of various crude oil and products to balance system supplies is necessary.

Energy futures contracts are used by large integrated oil companies to provide accessibility and visibility of market prices for the purchase and sale of physical oil. Liquidity in the futures markets ensures that specific hedging strategies can be successfully processed. Production can set forward sales prices. Refining operations can be hedged using crack spreads to set profit margins by fixing differentials between crude oil and product prices. In addition, margins on the distribution of petroleum products can be set.

The advent of options on underlying crude and heating oil futures contracts (see chapter 8) has introduced the concept of the "managed hedge" at a known cost—that is, the premium. Options provide the ability to hedge crude and heating oil cash and futures positions against adverse price movements without forgoing all the benefits of favorable price movements. Options also allow a company to fine-tune a hedge by allowing a choice of hedging insurance at different levels, costs, and degrees of protection.

An interview with the marketing and trading executives of three oil companies—Phillips Petroleum Company, CITGO Petroleum Corporation, and Conoco, Inc.—provides some insights into the manner in which the petroleum industry uses the futures market.

Phillips Petroleum Company is active in petroleum exploration and production on a worldwide basis with petroleum refining and marketing operations in the United States. As operations managers have become more familiar with the hedging tools available and the appropriate risk strategies to implement, participation in the futures and options markets has increased. The company entered the market in order to maintain a competitive edge as oil markets were deregulated and as volatility became more visible. Phillips found that the futures markets provided an index for price discovery and immediate market information. Liquidity in the NYMEX markets provided the company with the necessary flexibility and ease of entry and exit in order to process specific hedging transactions. The company hedges crude and heating oil cash and futures positions against adverse price changes without forgoing all the benefits of favorable price movements. Options provide insurance at a limited known cost. The company's current hedges include: (a) refinery supply crude prices, (b) purchase/sales for supply, and (c) inventories in tankage.

Phillips continues to formally segregate trading operations. Formal strategy meetings, however, are held twice a week with supply, refining, and marketing personnel to discuss open positions and proposed hedging strategies. At the same time, frequent informal contacts between traders and supply/marketing staff are maintained. In order to maintain the appropriate operational and accounting controls for its futures and options hedging program, the trading department reports directly to the vice president of supply and transportation.

CITGO Petroleum Corporation, a petroleum refining, marketing, and transportation company, is jointly owned by the Southland Corporation and Petróleos de Venezuela, S.A., each with a 50 percent equity interest. CITGO operates a 320,000 b/d high-conversion refinery at Lake Charles, Louisiana. It also operates a wholesale marketing operation primarily for gasoline and distillate fuels, which consists of forty-one equity-owned refined product terminals. Gasoline sales take place in forty-two states through 2,600 of Southland's 7-Eleven convenience stores and 5,400 jobber outlets. CITGO also markets jet fuel, distillates, lubricants, and other petroleum products. CITGO initially used futures as a hedging mechanism against physical product inventory in New York Harbor. Today the company uses futures to hedge crude, refined products, intermediate feedstocks, and blending components in New York Harbor, the U.S. Gulf Coast, and Chicago. Additionally, futures are used to supplement cash purchases/sales, to minimize basis risk either on a location or product basis, and to lock in transportation economics when delivering system product supplies. CITGO also utilizes options. Heating oil options are used to protect physical heating oil inventories through the purchase of puts, and/or to enhance cash flow by selling covered calls.

Conoco, Inc., is a major integrated oil firm and operates as a subsidiary of Dupont. Conoco's petroleum exploration and production activities include the production of crude oil in the United States and Canada and in the North Sea, Middle East, Africa, and Indonesia. Petroleum refining, marketing, and transportation operations are also conducted by Conoco. Conoco manufactures and sells a wide range of petroleum products, which include gasoline, jet fuel, and diesel fuel for transportation markets; distillate; and residual fuel oil, asphalt, and petrochemical feedstocks. The company sells gasoline and other refined products through retail outlets in forty-one U.S. states. As a result of an uncertain pricing environment, more intense competition among firms in the industry, and decreasing margins, Conoco needed a vehicle to manage increased price risk and price discovery and surveillance. Conoco began using heating oil futures in the early 1980s but found crude oil options a more flexible instrument for hedging. Conoco, as an oil producer, purchases put options to protect its cash or futures position against a price decline. Conoco also uses options to implement strategies specific to its own wet-barrel delivery system. For example, the company sells in-the-money options on expectations of buying futures that will be delivered into their Oklahoma system via an exchange of futures for physicals (EFP). At the same time, the company sells options against oil inventories to earn premium income. The company also incorporates options into marketing programs by guaranteeing price ceilings for their customers.

CHAPTER 7

The Rules of the Game

ORGANIZATION OF A COMMODITY EXCHANGE

To participate in futures trading, one cannot merely walk into a futures exchange and begin making bids and offers on futures contracts. One must be a member of the exchange to be able to engage in such transactions.

A commodity exchange is a voluntary association of people whose business involves, among other things, trading in commodity futures contracts. Most of these exchanges have developed out of organizations trading in spot markets. Thus, each exchange has its own history and tradition and each is independent of the others. The primary aim of a futures exchange is to provide and regulate a trading place so that its members (and through them, other interested parties) have the facility to buy or sell futures contracts for specific commodities.

Exchanges are often referred to as nonprofit organizations. They provide facilities that their members can use to make a profit, but the association itself is not organized to make money. Membership in U.S. exchanges is limited to individuals—that is, no memberships are held by companies. Each exchange has a certain number of members, and only these individuals are allowed to trade in futures contracts. Since the number of seats is fixed (occasionally the number may be adjusted by the board of directors), the only way to enter the association is to buy someone else's membership. Seats on some active exchanges are very valuable and are sometimes sold for several hundred thousand dollars.

The person interested in buying, however, should first apply to the membership committee of the exchange and, if the application is approved, may then proceed to purchase the seat.

Many people buy a membership in an exchange not because they want to get on the floor and trade, but because the commission cost is lower for members even when they are not present at the market and are represented by an agent. That is, if two individuals, one a member and one a nonmember, hire a broker, the nonmember pays a higher commission than the member. Although memberships are held by individuals, many of them are, in effect, administered by companies. Most members are employees of companies whose business involves futures trading.

Once an applicant becomes a member of an exchange, he can enter the exchange's trading floor (the pit) of the commodity he wants to trade (there are special trading hours for each commodity) and make a bid or offer. The first person who accepts the bid or offer will get the trade. Observers at each pit oversee the trading and note the prices at which trades are made. These observers record the prices and feed them into their communications systems. Prices are then almost instantaneously displayed on the boards and are also communicated to the brokerage offices and commodity firms all over the world. When a trade is made, each of the traders makes a note on a card of the price, quantity, delivery month, and the person with whom the trade was made. This record is submitted on a daily basis to the clearinghouse for reconciliation.

THE CLEARINGHOUSE

Each commodity exchange has its own clearinghouse. The members of the clearinghouse are not necessarily the same as the members of the exchange. Owning a seat on the exchange entitles a person to trade on the exchange floor. Any deal he makes, however, has to be registered with the clearinghouse through a clearinghouse member, each of whom has an account with the house. Upon notification of the deal, the clearinghouse member then files a report with the house of the transactions that should be included in its account. After these transactions are checked to see if they agree with the trading recorded on the floor, the clearinghouse becomes the "other party" to all buyers and sellers. Thus, a trader in the futures market does not need to be concerned about who took the opposite side of his trade. Any time he decides to liquidate his contract, the trader can do so without seeking the agreement of the other party. The clearinghouse guarantees performance of all contracts under exchange rules.

An individual wanting to become a member of a clearinghouse has to satisfy relatively high standards of creditworthiness. This provides the clearinghouse with a strong financial basis. Each clearinghouse member is required to deposit an initial margin on his contract positions with the clearinghouse. In addition, each day the member must send the clearinghouse a variation margin on each outstanding net contract on which there has been a loss for that day. The clearinghouse has at its disposal all the deposited margins to satisfy its financial obligations. Furthermore, the clearinghouse can draw upon its "guaranteed fund," which is a financial reserve provided by all its members.

The clearinghouse provides a considerable facility to buyers and sellers in the futures markets. It should be noted, however, that all of its functions are performed within the context of an intermediary agent. Thus, the clearinghouse does not earn any profit or bear any loss because of the futures deals—it simply redistributes the money from losers to winners.

In short, individuals wanting to trade in a futures exchange have to act through a member of the exchange. That member can buy or sell futures contracts on the exchange floor. He may not, however, be a member of the clearinghouse. He should then register his trade through a "house member." After this is accomplished, a futures contract that declares the house member as one party and the clearinghouse as the other party is issued. In other words, unlike contracts in the spot market, futures contracts are not bilateral among traders; the clearinghouse acts as seller to every buyer and buyer to every seller (see Figure 7.1).

CHARACTERISTICS OF FUTURES CONTRACTS

As explained earlier, less than one percent of petroleum futures contracts ever reach maturity and are actually delivered. A futures contract is, however, a valid, enforceable agreement. If the seller or the buyer should choose to make or take delivery, he may do so. Thus, the terms of the contract have to be precise and explicit.

A futures contract is standardized with respect to four elements:

- The quantity to be delivered (for instance 1,000 barrels of oil)
- The quality or qualities to be delivered (for example, light sweet crude with less than 5 percent sulphur content and gravity in the range of 34–45 °API)

Figure 7.1
How a Contract is Traded

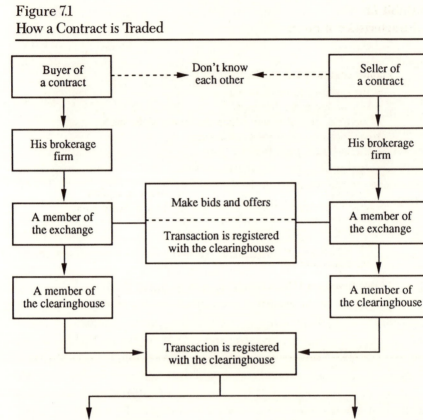

- The time interval within which delivery is to be made (for instance, the month of October)
- The location or locations where delivery can be made (for example, Cushing Storage, Oklahoma)

In addition to the above information, futures contracts contain a considerable amount of detailed description of the characteristics of the commodity and the method of delivery. For example, the crude oil (light sweet) contract traded on the NYMEX contains the following information.

Exhibit 7.1
Characteristics of Futures Contracts

Futures contracts are standardized with respect to
- the quantity to be delivered
- the quality to be delivered
- the time interval within which delivery is to be made
- the location or locations of delivery
- the method of delivery

They may include
- specific premiums or discounts for variations in quality
- specific premiums or discounts for different delivery points

They normally contain limits on
- the minimum price fluctuation
- the maximum permissible price fluctuation

The contracts on U.S. exchanges impose
- a limit on the number of contracts that each person can hold

---

First, with regard to the grade and quality of crude, the contract states that the crude's viscosity should be 325 (or less) seconds Saybolt Universal; its vapor pressure should be less than 9.5 pounds per square inch at 100°F; its basic sediment (water and other impurities) should be less than one percent; and its pour point should not exceed 50°F. The acceptable stream designations are: U.K. Brent Blend, Nigerian Brass Blend, and Bonny Light; Norwegian Ekofisk; Tunisian Zarzaitine; Algerian Saharan Blend; and Texas Intermediate, and Mid and South Texas Sweet. The par crude is West Texas Intermediate with gravity of 40 °API and 0.4 percent sulphur content. If the gravity is less than that of the par crude, there will be a $0.02/b discount under the contract price for each degree gravity below par. (There will be no gravity adjustment if the gravity is above par.) If the sulphur content of the stream designation is different from that of the par crude, there will be a $0.05/b premium (discount) over (under) the contract price for each tenth of a percentage point of sulphur content less (greater) than par. Finally, delivery of Brass Blend, Bonny Light, and Saharan Blend will entail a $0.25/b premium over par.

Second, with regard to price fluctuations, the contract contains a set of rules that aim at initiating the trade within a manageable range of price fluctuations and extending this range as the market develops the capacity to absorb wider fluctuations.

These rules are:

(a) The maximum permissible price fluctuation in any day is $1.00/b above or below the preceding day's settling price (this is called the basic maximum fluctuation).

(b) If the settling price for any month exceeds the basic maximum fluctuation in either direction, the maximum permissible fluctuation in either direction for all months during the next business session will be expanded by 50 percent of the basic maximum fluctuation above the basic maximum fluctuation.

(c) If the settling price for any month during a business session for which the maximum permissible fluctuation has been expanded does not move by the said expanded maximum fluctuation, the maximum permissible fluctuation for the next business session will be set back to the basic maximum fluctuation.

(d) If the settling price changes within the expanded permissible fluctuation, the maximum permissible fluctuation will be expanded again by 100 percent of the basic maximum fluctuation above the basic maximum fluctuation.

(e) If the settling price does not fluctuate by this twice-expanded range, the maximum permissible fluctuation will be set back to the initially expanded range (to 50 percent above the basic).

(f) There will be no maximum limit on price fluctuations during the month preceding the delivery month.

Thus, rule (a) establishes the initial range, and rules (b), (d), and (f) determine how this range is expanded. Rules (c) and (e) indicate the conditions under which the range of price fluctuation will be set back to its previous level.

Third, the contract imposes a limitation on holdings of futures contracts. This is very important from the viewpoint of the economics of oil futures because the limitation is aimed at barring the development of monopoly power in the market. According to the contract, no person should own or control a net long or net short position in light crude petroleum in any one month, or in all months combined, of more than 5,000 contracts. In addition, in the month preceding a delivery month, no person should own or control a net long or net short position of more than 750 contracts in light crude for the delivery month. The contract also takes a precautionary step by stating that the positions of all accounts owned or controlled by a person or persons acting in concert shall be cumulative. The exception to this rule is the case of a so-called bona fide hedger. If a hedger can show that the hedge is necessary or advisable as an integral part of his business (i.e., it is not a speculative act), his limit will be raised to 10,000 contracts in any one month or in all months combined, and to 3,000 contracts in the month preceding the delivery month.

Fourth, with regard to the delivery procedure (see Figure 7.2), the contract provides that trading in the current delivery month shall cease on the fifth business day prior to the twenty-fifth calendar day of the month preceding the delivery month. A member who has a long position has to give the clearinghouse a "notice of intention to accept delivery" by noon on the first business day after the final day of trading. This notice should indicate the number of contracts to be accepted, the buyer's preferred outgoing pipeline or preferred storage facility and his preference of light "sweet" crude oil by origin, sulphur content, and API gravity. In the same manner, a member who has a short position has to give the clearinghouse a delivery notice by noon on the first business day after the final day of trading. This notice should indicate the number of contracts to be delivered, and the origin, sulphur content, and API gravity of the light "sweet" crude oil to be delivered.

The clearinghouse will match the notices coming from both sides and determine the corresponding parties. The seller will then have until the last business day of the month preceding the delivery month to give the buyer a "scheduling notice" in which the seller states delivery time. The buyer and seller are, of course, free to change (by mutual agreement) the delivery terms with respect to the method of delivery, timing of delivery, type of crude to be delivered, and designation of buyer's and/or seller's facility. In any event, after the delivery is arranged, the buyer must pay the seller by noon on the twentieth calendar day following the delivery month, and the seller must give the buyer the pipeline ticket and all other certificates and documents required for the transfer of title.

SPECIFICS OF PETROLEUM CONTRACTS

Petroleum futures contracts have a variety of technical and commercial specifications that are specifically designed by each exchange for

Figure 7.2
How the Delivery is Made

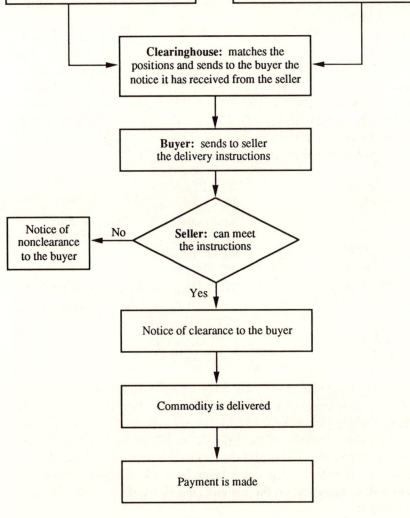

The clearing member with long position: sends to the clearinghouse information on the names of his customers, the number of contracts, and the preferred site of delivery

The clearing member with short position: sends to the clearinghouse information on the names of his customers, the number of contracts, and the location of supply

Clearinghouse: matches the positions and sends to the buyer the notice it has received from the seller

Buyer: sends to seller the delivery instructions

Seller: can meet the instructions

No → Notice of nonclearance to the buyer

Yes ↓

Notice of clearance to the buyer

Commodity is delivered

Payment is made

each underlying commodity. The specifications of several contracts, which provide representative samples of almost all petroleum futures contracts, are reviewed in this section.

Petroleum Contracts Traded at NYMEX

As discussed in chapter 6, NYMEX has played a leading role in U.S. petroleum futures trading in recent years. Its first successful contract was the New York Harbor heating oil contract, which began trading in November 1978.

The heating oil contract unit is 42,000 U.S. gallons (1,000 barrels). Its delivery location is New York Harbor, which, for the purpose of the contract, includes the area of New York Harbor extending from the East River west of Hunts Point; the Narrows, the Lower Bay west of Norton Point, the Newark Bay, the Hackensack River and Passaic River south of the Pulaski Skyway Bridge, the Kill Van Kul, the Arthur Kill, and the Raritan River east of the Garden State Parkway Bridge.

The quality specifications of the heating oil are:

Gravity:	30 °API minimum
Flash:	130° minimum
Viscosity:	Kinematic, Centistokes at 100°F, minimum 2.0, maximum 3.6
Water and sediment:	0.05 maximum
Pour point:	0°F maximum
Distillation:	10% point, 480°F maximum; 90% point, 640°F maximum; end point 670°F maximum
Sulphur:	0.2% maximum
Color:	maximum 2.5

Delivery has to be made FOB seller's New York Harbor facility with all duties, fees, and other charges paid by the seller. The buyer has the option of taking the delivery into his barge or truck, into tanker or pipeline, as a stock transfer of the title, or as an intrafacility transfer and interfacility transfer of the oil if the facility used by the seller and buyer allows such transfer. If delivery is taken by truck, the buyer should pay a per-gallon surcharge on the amount, which would be determined by the exchange.

Following the success of the New York Harbor heating oil contract, NYMEX introduced in August 1981 another heating oil contract for delivery in the Gulf Coast area. This contract contains the same provisions with regard to contract unit and quality specifications. The major difference is, of course, the delivery location. In this contract, the delivery is made in the Gulf Coast area, which extends from Pasadena, Harris County (Texas), to Collins, Covington County (Mississippi), and includes facilities located in Brazoria County (Texas) and Jackson County (Mississippi), both of which have access to Colonial Pipeline injection points in Pasadena (Texas) and Collins (Mississippi). As mentioned previously, this contract is not active at present.

Gasoline (leaded and unleaded) contracts were introduced on NYMEX in October 1981. The contract unit is 42,000 U.S. gallons (1,000 barrels), and the delivery location is New York Harbor. The unleaded gasoline should meet the following standards of quality:

Gravity:	52 °API minimum
Color:	undyed
Corrosion:	3 hours at 122°, maximum 1
Lead:	maximum 0.03 grams per gallon
Doctor:	negative or, if necessary, Mercaptan Sulphur: weight percent, maximum 0.002
Octane:	RON, minimum 91.0; MON, minimum 82.0; (RON + MON)/2 minimum 87 and maximum less than 91.0

Reid vapor maximum pounds, January, February—14.5, pressure: March, April—13.5, May, June, July, August, September—11.5, October, November—13.5, December—14.5

Northern Grade	Class			
December, January, February	E			
March, April, October, November	D			
May, September	C			
June, July, August	C			
	B	C	D	E
10% evaporation °F maximum	149,	140,	131,	122
50% evaporation °F maximum	170,	170,	170,	170
50% evaporation °F maximum	245,	240,	235,	230
90% evaporation °F maximum	374,	365,	365,	365

End point °F maximum   430,   430, 430, 430

The standards of quality of leaded regular gasoline are the same as the above, except for

Color:	orange or bronze in sufficient quantity to meet U.S. Surgeon General's minimum requirements
Lead:	maximum 4 grams per gallon
Octane:	RON, minimum 91.5; MON, Report; (RON + MON)/2 minimum 89.0

Prices of both contracts are quoted in dollars and cents per gallon. The minimum price fluctuation is \$0.01 per gallon. The maximum permissible price fluctuation in any one day is \$0.02 per gallon above or below the preceding day's settling price (called the "basic maximum fluctuation"). The maximum price fluctuation may be extended under special circumstances. If the settling price for any month passes the basic maximum fluctuation in either direction, the maximum permissible fluctuation for all months during the next business session will be expanded by 50 percent of the basic maximum fluctuation above the basic maximum fluctuation. The maximum permissible fluctuation may again be expanded if the price change hits the new limit. There is, however, no maximum limit on price fluctuations during the month preceding the delivery month. This is to ensure that the futures price at the maturity date converges with the spot market price.

Trading of the current month's futures contracts will cease on the last business day of the month preceding the delivery month. By noon on the first business day of the delivery month, both buyers (clearing members having open long positions) and sellers (clearing members having open short positions) must file with the exchange the forms prescribed by the exchange. The buyer will provide information regarding the names of his customers, the number of contracts, and preferred site of delivery. The seller will file a form, called a "delivery notice," with the exchange which provides the number of contracts, the names of his customers, and the name and location of the facility that will supply the product.

The clearinghouse of the exchange will match the size of the positions and will send the buyer the delivery notice that it has received from the seller. The buyer is then obliged to give to the seller (identified in the delivery notice) the initial delivery instructions. The seller will then give the buyer a notice of clearance, indicating that he is prepared to make delivery in accordance with the buyer's delivery instructions, or he must give the buyer a notice of "nonclearance" and state the reason for such inability. He may, at his option, in the notice of nonclearance suggest an alternative delivery site and/or a preferred delivery date or time. A copy of all communications between the buyer and the seller goes to the exchange.

All deliveries must be completed after the fifth business day and before the last business day of the delivery month. For purposes of the contract, shipment is said to commence when the product passes the buyer's cargo intake flange, tank, or pipeline connection, at which point the buyer assumes the risk of loss. Finally, the buyer pays the seller at the office of the seller by certified check by noon of the business day following receipt of the product. The amount of the payment is based on the volume delivered as determined at 60°F.

The contract provides some flexibility with respect to delivery. The seller and buyer (matched by the exchange) may agree to make and take delivery under terms and conditions that differ from those contained in the contract. In such a case, the buyer and seller execute an "alternative delivery notice" on the form prescribed by the exchange and deliver a completed copy of such notice to the exchange. This action will release the buyer, the seller, and the exchange from their respective obligations under the contract. Upon receipt of the notice, the exchange will return to the buyer and seller all margin monies held in their respective accounts with respect to the contracts, and the exchange is indemnified against any liability, cost, or expense associated with the execution, delivery, or performance of the agreement between the seller and the buyer.

PETROLEUM CONTRACTS TRADED AT THE INTERNATIONAL PETROLEUM EXCHANGE

IPE is organized somewhat differently from U.S. commodity exchanges. The difference is due to the types of membership of the exchange and the relationship between the exchange and the clearinghouse. Membership of IPE falls into two categories:

• Floor membership with voting rights;
• Associate membership with no voting rights.

To become a "floor member," a trader must have a London office and minimum assets of £20,000 (US$30,000). The floor member does not pay any commission on the trade and has the right to vote.

Associate members consist of two groups. The first group includes trade members who are, principally, established oil trading companies. They pay a membership fee and participate in futures trading through a floor member, but they pay a lower commission than those who are not members of the exchange. The second group includes general associate members, who are mostly small companies and speculators. They cannot qualify for trade membership, but they are permitted to trade through floor members.

The relationship between IPE and its clearinghouse is of interest because the clearinghouse is completely independent from IPE. The International Commodities Clearing-House Limited has been providing futures markets in London with clearing services since its formation in 1888. It is now providing IPE with clearing services. Its operation is similar to that of U.S. clearinghouses. It serves as a counterpart to each seller or buyer of a futures contract. It guarantees all contracts on the market and acts as an intermediary to arrange delivery should a contract reach its maturity date.

The first contract introduced on IPE, which began trading in April 1981, was one for gasoil futures. The contract unit is 100 tonnes, and the delivery locations are at specific tank installations in the Amsterdam, Rotterdam, and Antwerp (ARA) area. The contract price is quoted in U.S. dollars and cents per tonne, and payment is made in the same currency in London. The minimum price fluctuation is $0.25 per tonne ($25.00 per contract); the maximum price variation in each trading session is $30.00 per tonne. If the price varies by $30.00 per tonne from the previous day's price, trading will cease for half an hour. It will then begin with no maximum limit on the price fluctuation.

The quality specifications of the IPE gasoil contract are:

Density at 15°C:	0.855 kg per liter maximum
Color:	2.0 ASTM maximum
Flash point:	55°C minimum
Total sulphur:	0.3% maximum
Cloud point:	-2°C maximum
Cold filter plugged point:	-9°C maximum.

Trading of the current month's contract ends on the last business day of the month preceding delivery. If a contract reaches the maturity date, delivery must take place between the fourteenth and the last day of the delivery month.

Encouraged by the success of the gasoil contract, IPE introduced a crude oil contract in November 1983. The contract became dormant shortly afterwards, but a revised contract was introduced in 1988. The contract calls for delivery of a crude within a range of gravity of 35–45 °API with a maximum sulphur content of 0.4 percent. The par crude is Brent Blend. Ninian Blend, Forties Blend, Ekofisk, Bonny Light, Brass River, Zarzaitine, and Saharan Blend are also deliverable, with appropriate premiums or discounts applicable. The choice of Brent Blend as the market crude facilitates trade because it is the largest crude volume traded on the European market. Furthermore, its similarities to West Texas Intermediate (the par crude on NYMEX) and Light Louisiana Sweet (the par crude on CBT) encourages the simultaneous purchase and sale of futures (arbitrage) between IPE and the U.S. exchanges.

The quality specifications of the IPE crude oil contract are:

Gravity:	35-45 °API
Sulphur:	0.4% maximum
Pour point:	50°F maximum
Viscosity:	Kinematic, Centistokes at 50°C, 45 maximum
Metals:	25 parts per million, maximum
Bottom sediment and water:	1% maximum
Reid vapor pressure:	10 lbs per square inch, maximum.

The contract unit is 1,000 barrels (as opposed to the gasoil futures, which were in units of 100 tonnes). Delivery is made in the Rotterdam/Amsterdam area, FOB ship, by intertank transfer, by in-tank transfer, or "free in pipeline" at the buyer's option. When deliveries are less than fifty lots (contracts), however, delivery is made by in-tank transfer. Furthermore, if the buyer and seller agree on an alternative delivery procedure during the month prior to the delivery month, any location or crude may be used at agreed discounts or premiums.

The contract price is quoted in dollars and cents per barrel, and payment is made in U.S. dollars in London. The minimum price fluctuation is $0.01/b.

INTRODUCTION OF PROPANE AND NATURAL GAS CONTRACTS

The instability of oil prices has led to an increased volatility in other energy prices, which, in turn, has forced producers, distributors, and consumers of all energy products to seek ways to protect themselves against unfavorable price movements. In response, NYMEX developed a propane contract, which was introduced in 1987, and a natural gas contract, which was introduced in 1990.

Propane Contract

The propane contract calls for 42,000 U.S. gallons of propane at Mont Belvieu, Texas. Mont Belvieu is known as the center of propane spot trading in the United States. It is the point of origin for the Texas Eastern Transmission Pipeline, which serves the midwestern, eastern, and southeastern United States. The Dixie Pipeline, serving the Gulf Coast and southern states, also originates in Mont Belvieu.

One of the important features of the propane contract is its delivery mechanism. Trading of the contract terminates on the last business day preceding the delivery month. No later than an hour before trading terminates, all remaining shorts (parties who have sold contracts that have not been offset and who are therefore obligated to make delivery) must certify to their clearing members that they will have at a bona fide delivery facility the quantity of propane necessary for delivery by the first delivery day. All deliveries are FOB any pipeline, storage, or fractionation facility in Mont Belvieu, Texas, with direct access to Texas Eastern Products Pipeline. On the first business day after the termination of trading, all customers are given several hours to arrange an exchange of futures for physicals (EFP) if they so desire. Through an EFP, participants on opposite sides of the market can swap cash and futures and make arrangements for subsequent delivery under circumstances in which all terms (price, location, grade, timing) are fully negotiable. By 2:00 P.M. of that day, both the long and short customer (through their clearing members) must file with the exchange a "petroleum product notice." Besides basic customer information (name of the short clearing member's customer, number of contracts, tender number of the matched transaction, etc.), the petroleum product notice enables the short clearing member's customer to designate the delivery facility and the long clearing member's customer to indicate the preferred delivery facilities and preference of delivery mode (i.e., in storage, book transfer, etc.). While the exchange's clearing department does not guarantee that the long will be assigned to the delivery facility requested, it will make efforts to match parties according to the preferences contained in the petroleum product notice. On the second business day of the delivery month the exchange will inform each long and short clearing member who will be on the other side of the delivery and which delivery facility has been designated. As soon as possible, but not later than the fourth business day of the delivery month, the long must inform the short (and confirm in writing) of the precise details of the delivery (name, number of contracts, etc.) and, most importantly, of the ten-day window in which delivery is to be made.

All movement of propane (physical or otherwise) must take place in the designated window, and windows can only be designated from the tenth calendar day to two business days before the end of the delivery month. Prior to informing the short clearing member of the details, the long clearing member must contact the scheduler at the designated facility to ensure that the facility can accommodate the delivery request. In a pump-over or interfacility transfer, the short provides the long with the final details of the delivery, including the date and approximate time the pump-over will begin. This must be done at least three days prior to the initiation of the pump-over, and the exchange must be given a copy of the instructions.

Natural Gas Contract

Consideration of a natural gas futures contract began in 1983 when it became clear that certain categories of natural gas would be deregulated on January 1, 1985. On this date, wellhead prices for most new gas—drilled on or after February 19, 1977—were removed from price control, thus affecting an estimated 60 percent of available natural gas supplies. The early NYMEX proposed contract was based on the intrastate market in Texas, since Texas has the greatest gas production and consumption in the United States. The intrastate market was selected because, in 1984, interstate transportation service was not widely available. After the Federal Energy Regulatory Commission (FERC) instituted the Order 436 program in October 1985 and the interstate market became more accessible, NYMEX modified its proposal. In the new version of the contract, Katy, Texas (southwest of Houston), was selected as the delivery location, largely due to its proximity to interstate and intrastate pipeline interconnections and access to most Texas supply and consumption areas.

In 1986 and 1987, the exchange continued to refine its proposed contract and worked with pipelines in the Katy, Texas, area to develop a mechanism through which deliveries could be carried out under the futures contract. These efforts resulted in the creation of the Katy Interchange Service, which will provide delivery service for futures and cash transactions through access to the Katy area facilities via the following pipelines: Transcontinental Gas Pipe Line Corp., Trunkline Gas Co., Coronado Transmission Co., and Yankee Pipeline Co. Interchange service will begin when natural gas enters a designated point within the Katy interchange and will end when gas is delivered through the final outgoing interchange point. Yankee Pipeline Co. has been selected by the participants to serve as the operator of the Katy interchange and will coordinate the transfer of gas through the interchange. The seller is responsible for transporting the gas to the interchange; the buyer has responsibility for arranging transportation from the outgoing point of the interchange. On December 9, 1987, the above pipeline participants jointly filed an application with the FERC to establish the Katy Interchange Service.

The NYMEX natural gas futures contract includes the following specifications:

Trading unit:	10,000 million Btu. Delivery tolerance of 2% above or below contract unit.
Delivery location:	Katy, Texas.
Quality specifications:	Interchange service in effect at the time of delivery.
Delivery months:	Such months as shall be determined by the NYMEX board of directors.
Minimum fluctuations:	$0.001 per million Btu. ($10.00 per contract).
Price limits:	$0.10 per million Btu. ($1,000 per contract). No maximum limit on the nearby (spot) contract.
Termination of trading:	On the third business day prior to the twenty-fifth calendar day of the month preceding the delivery month.

CHAPTER 8

Petroleum Options Trading

Although petroleum futures, and in particular crude oil contracts, provide powerful instruments for managing the risk associated with price fluctuations, there are at least two areas in which further flexibility is desired. First, futures contracts extend over a fairly short period of time; trading is normally active only for contracts of up to six-month maturity. Second, hedging with a futures contract involves committing to a fixed price regardless of forthcoming events in the market. Options trading, on the other hand, provides a bit more flexibility, particularly in the second area. Options can be used independently or in conjunction with futures contracts, providing a wide range of possibilities for managing risk in petroleum trading.

Option trading, in a general sense, dates back to the seventeenth century, when the Dutch used options in the notorious tulip bulb craze. Tulip merchants bought promises of delivery from the growers to protect themselves against fluctuating prices. This promise would obligate the farmer to sell the tulips at a predetermined price, but would not obligate the merchant to buy the tulips. For the merchant, the arrangement provided a right to buy for which he would pay a premium. If the price of tulips declined, the option would be worthless, but the tulips could then be purchased in the marketplace at a lower price.

Modern-day option trading has existed for decades in over-the-counter markets for many stocks in the United States. Before 1973, however, options had not been standardized. The exercise price was usually set at the current market price and the option period was typically three, six, or nine months. So, at any time and on any stock, the previously traded options made up numerous expiration dates and covered a wide range of exercise prices. This meant that, for all practical purposes, the original market makers were the only potential buyers in a rather makeshift secondary options market. There was not much opportunity to resell the options. In April 1973, all this changed when the Chicago Board Options Exchange (CBOE) came into existence with its new "standardized" options. The opening of this exchange was soon followed by the opening of the American, Pacific, and Philadelphia stock exchanges.

Over time, option trading expanded to cover a wide variety of stocks and futures contracts. In the case of petroleum, the need for option trading emerged with the increasing volatility of the spot price. Initially this increasing volatility triggered some companies, including Morgan Stanley, Philbro, and Standard Oil, to offer their own tailor-made options during 1985–86. The formal trading of petroleum options started on November 14, 1986, when NYMEX introduced its option on crude oil futures. This action was then followed by the opening of options on heating oil and unleaded gasoline futures contracts.

MECHANICS OF OPTION TRADING

The first step towards understanding how option trading works is to become familiar with the jargon—calls, puts, premiums, strike price, etc.

In any option trading, one side reserves the right (with no obligation) to transact the business, while the other side accepts the obligation to transact the business if asked to. The person who reserves the right is the buyer of the option; the person who accepts the obligation is the writer of the option. The buyer of the option should, of course, pay a premium for reserving the right to do the business, and the writer of the option receives that premium in return for committing himself to the business transaction. The business itself can be a purchase or a sale of a commodity, a stock, or a futures contract. Thus the buyer of an option can be buying the right to purchase or the right to sell. What he is buying is the right to transact the deal. When he reserves a right to purchase, he is said to be buying a "call option." On the other hand, when he reserves the right to sell, he is said to be buying a "put option." For each of these options, there should be an "option writer," that is, a person who accepts the obligation (to sell or to purchase) in exchange for a premium. To avoid the normal confusions, one should note that call options and put options are not complementary; the buying of a call option does not necessitate transacting a put option on behalf of the other side of the deal. When a call option is bought, the other side "writes" the call option. That is, one side buys the right to purchase and the other side sells this right. The buyer of the right to purchase is, in fact, paying a premium to acquire a special privilege: if the price increases, the benefit lies in the exercise of the option—the contract can be bought at a prior fixed price; if the price falls, nothing will be lost because there is no requirement to buy—the option simply expires. The only cost, therefore, is the premium paid; whatever the market does, either something is gained or nothing is lost. The writer of the call option receives the premium to put himself in an especially disadvantageous position: if the price goes up, he will lose because he has to sell the underlying stock or futures to the buyer of the option at a prior fixed price; if the price drops, the option writer will not gain because the buyer of the option will not be buying the stock any longer. So, for the option writer, the only gain is the premium he has received; whatever the market does, he either loses something or wins nothing.

If the option writer actually owns the underlying stock or futures, it is called a "covered" write. Otherwise, it is called a "naked" write to emphasize the added exposure of being called to deliver the stock or futures. The naked option writer is similar to the short seller in the futures market in the sense that they both are selling something that they do not own.

In addition to the similarities between futures and options, it is also useful to note the contrasts between the two methods. In the futures market, transactions fall into one of the following two categories: (1) a commodity is purchased for future delivery; or (2) a commodity is sold for future delivery. In option trading, however, a transaction could fall into one of the following four categories: (1) the right to purchase a commodity is bought (buyer of a call option); (2) the obligation to sell a commodity is sold (the writer of a call option); (3) the right to sell a commodity is bought (buyer of a put option); or (4) the obligation to buy a commodity is sold (seller of a put option). But it is important to note that for each transaction only two parties are involved. Each transaction is either a trade between (1) and (2) or a trade between (3) and (4). In other words, a call option is a transaction that is totally independent from a put option, and neither of the two needs to be done in conjunction with the other. Indeed, most option transactions are call options, and there is normally a smaller number of put options traded on the stock or futures exchanges of the United States.

The next step in comparing options trading with futures contracts is to contrast their profit and loss mechanisms. It is worthwhile to recall that the commitments involved in a futures contract are symmetrical for the buyer and the seller. Both have to meet their commitments even when it is not profitable for them to do so. By contrast, an option buyer will only exercise his right when it is profitable for him to do so; the option writer has no choice but to meet his obligation. Thus, the premium paid by the buyer of an option contract is to compensate for the asymmetry between the buyer's rights and the seller's obligations.

For example, a trader purchases a call option for August crude at $16.00/b. He will pay, say, $0.50/b as premium to reserve the right to buy this contract. If the price of the contract rises to $18.00/b, he would exercise the option and make $2.00/b gross profit on the contract. From this gross profit, $0.50/b has to be deducted to arrive at the net profit of $1.50/b for this trader. The writer (seller) of the option would lose $2.00/b on the contract, but because he has received $0.50 as premium, his net loss will be $1.50/b.

Carrying this further, it can be assumed that after the purchase of the call option, the August crude contract falls to $14.00/b. Obviously, the purchaser of the call option will not exercise his option; he will let it expire because he can buy crude on the spot market at a price lower than $16.00, which is the strike price of his option. Thus, his loss is limited to $0.50/b (the premium he paid) even though the price has actually declined by $2.00. The writer (seller) of the option will gain only $0.50/b —the premium he received when he sold the option. In summary, the purchaser of this call option will exercise his option only if the August crude trades above $16.00/b. If the crude does trade above $16.00/b, his net profit will be the gross profit minus the premium of $0.50. Thus, he will make a net profit only if the price exceeds $16.50/b. The seller of the option would have to deliver his obligation only when the buyer wants him to— that is, when the price is above $16.00/b and the seller is bound to lose because of the delivery. Thus, at a price above $16.00/b, the buyer profits and the seller loses; there is no limit to this gain and loss. At a price below $16.00/b, the buyer does not lose more than the premium he has paid and the seller will not gain more than that premium.

The main difference between the reward systems of futures contracts and options trading is in the structure of price risk for sellers and buyers of contracts. In the case of a futures contract, both the buyer and the seller can have unlimited gain or loss depending on price variations. In the case of options, the buyer has the possibility of unlimited gain, but his loss will not exceed the paid premium. The seller faces the possibility of unlimited loss, but his gain will not exceed the premium. It may appear that the buyer of an option is in a better position, which may cause some to wonder why some people would want to be option sellers. It is clearly not true that the buyer of an option has the better position. What more or less equalizes, at least in a probabilistic sense, the positions of buyers and sellers is the size of the premium.

WHAT FACTORS DETERMINE THE SIZE OF THE PREMIUM?

In general, the premium that a purchaser of, say, a call option, is willing to pay depends on his judgment about the possibility and the extent to which the price of the underlying stock or commodity will move above the strike price of the option. More specifically, the premium depends on the following factors:

- The difference between the strike price of the option and the current price of the stock or commodity;
- The expected volatility of the price of the stock or commodity;
- The time of expiration of the option;
- The level of risk-free interest rates.

The first factor, the difference between the current price of a futures contract and the strike price of the option on that contract, represents the minimum premium for an option. It indicates the relative position of the bet. For example, buying a call option with a strike price of $14.00/b for an August crude oil futures contract while the current price of the August crude contract is $16.00/b is very favorably positioned. What has happened is that the right to buy the August contract at $14.00/b at any instant from now till the expiration date of the option has been reserved. The difference between $16.00/b and $14.00/b is referred to as the "intrinsic value" and represents the minimum premium for the option because this minimum value can be received immediately. That is, the option can be exercised immediately, if so desired, which means that an August crude oil futures contract at the price of $14.00/b is bought while the current price of the same contract is $16.00/b. If a decision is made not to exercise the option now, it is because of the expectation that prices will go up further and the option will be worth more than $2.00/b some time in the future but before the expiration date of the option contract.

The second factor, price volatility, is the main incentive for option trading; with no price volatility, option trading would cease to exist. The greater the volatility, the greater the probable price range in the future. With a wider price range, the option buyer is more likely to profit and the option writer is more likely to lose. Therefore, there is a direct relationship between the option premium and the volatility of the price of the underlying commodity. In the discussion of futures contracts in earlier chapters, it was mentioned that price volatility was also essential for futures trading. There is, however, a fundamental difference between the impact of price volatility on futures trading and the impact of price volatility on options trading. In the case of futures contracts, price fluctuation represents a risk for both sides of the trade. In a market with a wide range of price fluctuation, both the buyer and the seller of a futures contract take a risk by committing to delivery of the commodity at a fixed price because, by the time of delivery, the market price may be substantially higher or lower than the fixed price agreed under a futures contract. In the case of an option contract, price volatility represents a benefit only to the purchaser and a risk only to the seller. If the market price fluctuates extensively and frequently, it is likely to hit a level favorable to the purchaser of the option, at which point he would immediately exercise the option and make a profit. With such fluctuations, the price is also likely to hit a level unfavorable to the buyer, but then he would not exercise the option. In short, price volatility plays a more important role in option trading than in futures trading because the reward system of the former is not symmetric. For the same reason, price volatility directly impacts the size of option premiums.

The third factor, the time of expiration of the option, affects the size of an option premium and also increases the probability that the market price will hit a level favorable to the buyer of the option. To exemplify, two call options—both on the same commodity (e.g., crude oil futures) and both with the same strike price (e.g., $18.00/b)—can be compared. The only difference is that the first option will expire in one month and the second option in two months. In the case of the first option, the buyer will profit if the price exceeds $18.00/b at any time during the next thirty days, whereas in the case of the second option, the buyer has the same opportunity, but for two months. Clearly, the second option offers a better profit potential and is worth more than the first option. Thus, other things being equal, the longer the period to the expiration date of an option, the larger is the size of its premium. For the same reason, the market value of an option contract (i.e., the premium) declines very rapidly as the option approaches its maturity. If the option is not exercised by the date of maturity, its value becomes zero.

The fourth factor, the level of risk-free interest rates, is less important than other factors in determining option premiums. The idea here is that when people buy options, they are indeed putting their capital in this use and thus giving up other investments. The risk-free interest rate is then used as an indication of the return on the alternative investment (opportunity cost). When interest rates change, people will alter their demand for option contracts, thereby affecting the option premium.

The above four factors affect the size of option premiums in a rather clear manner. A mathematical model introduced by Black and Scholes quantifies the relationship between the size of the premium and the strike price, the market price, the time to maturity, the interest rate, and price volatility (as measured by the variance of percentage change in price). The actual option premium is, of course, determined through the interactions of bids and offers on the pertinent exchange. The Black and Scholes formula provides an estimate of a "fair premium." A fair premium is one that may be viewed as an equilibrium premium—one that would equalize the return prospects, as estimated at the time of the trade, for both sides of an option contract. The Black-Scholes model is used for stock option pricing. A variation of this model, called the Black Model, along with several modified versions of it, are used in pricing options on futures.

The main difficulty in estimating an option premium is assessing market volatility. Simply defined, volatility represents the degree to which the underlying futures contract is likely to fluctuate—in either direction. It is measured by taking the standard deviation of daily price relatives—today's price relative to yesterday's price. There are, however, two ways to calculate volatility: on a historical basis or on an implied basis.

Historical volatility is that which is actually observed in the marketplace, most commonly over a ten-, twenty-, or thirty-day period. This process is a deductive means of calculating market volatility. Implied volatility is an inductive method. It backs out the volatility of the underlying futures contract from the market-traded option premium. Implied volatility is a barometer of expectations for the future rather than a measure of what has happened in the past. Estimations of future vol-

Table 8.1
Implied Volatility and Premium for Heating Oil Options

Strike price ($)	$0.43 Implied volatility (%)	$0.44 Option premium (%)	$0.45 Option delta	Option premium (%)	Delta	Premium	Delta
	25	.0179	64	.0248	75	.0327	84
0.42	30	.0202	62	.0269	72	.0344	80
	35	.0226	61	.0291	69	.0363	77
	25	.0082	39	.0127	51	.0184	63
0.44	30	.0106	41	.0152	52	.0209	62
	35	.0131	43	.0178	52	.0234	61
	25	.0031	19	.0054	28	.0088	40
0.46	30	.0049	23	.0076	32	.0113	42
	35	.0069	27	.0099	35	.0138	43

Source: Kay (1988).

atility can change erratically over short periods of time. Prior to the December 1987 OPEC meeting, for example, the implied volatility in crude oil jumped from a low of 15 percent to a high of 46 percent over only a couple of months. In general, implied volatility in the oil market has peaked with new price lows, indicating a clear bearish bias in the market.

Implied volatility is helpful in evaluating whether a particular option is fairly priced, overpriced, or underpriced in relation to other options or to other hedging alternatives. For example, if call options are pricing a significant increase in market volatility, their premiums may fall while underlying prices remain unchanged should volatility estimates suddenly fall. This can be seen by examining the premiums for each of three levels of implied volatility in Table 8.1. The potential sensitivity of option premiums to changing estimates of market volatility is clear.

Pricing models such as the Black Model assume that options will not be exercised prior to expiration. Of course, few option traders actually do so, owing to timing mismatches, time decay, and short-term profit opportunities. Thus, a common derivation of the Black Model measures something called the "delta."

Table 8.2
Value of Delta for Long Heating Oil Options

Futures price	$0.43	$0.44	$0.45
Buy $0.44 call	+0.41	+0.52	+0.62
Buy $0.44 put	−0.61	−0.49	−0.37

Source: Kay (1988).

Delta measures the sensitivity of option premiums to changes in underlying futures prices. Delta also represents the probability that a given option will have value at expiration, given current market prices and expectations about volatility. As such, delta is dynamic—it changes with any change in market prices or expectations.

Delta values range from zero for deep-out-of-the-money options to 1.0 for deep-in-the-money bullish positions and -1.0 for deep-out-of-the-money bearish positions. At-the-money options ordinarily have a delta of about plus (long calls) or minus (long puts) .5. To illustrate: a call option with a delta of .5 should move up $0.05 for a $0.10 upward move in the underlying futures contract. Deep-in-the-money options behave much like futures contracts, since they are almost certain to have value at expiration. Options that are deep-out-of-the-money show little or no response to movements in the underlying futures contract, since there is very little chance that they will have value at expiration, regardless of what futures prices do. Table 8.2, which shows the value of delta for long heating oil options, assumes an implied volatility of 25 percent and thirty-one days until option expiration. For a long option, call deltas are positive and put deltas are negative. As a call option moves further into the money, its delta increases until it eventually approaches 1.0. Meanwhile, a long put option's delta becomes more negative as the option moves further into the money, until it eventually reaches -1.0.

Deltas for short option positions work in reverse. A short call's delta becomes increasingly negative as the option moves further into the money. And a short put's delta becomes higher as the put moves further into the money. Two concepts to show the effect of changes in implied volatility on options deltas can be combined. While an increase in volatility has only a minor effect on at-the-money option deltas, it significantly increases out-of-the-money deltas and significantly decreases in-

Table 8.3
Equivalent Net Futures Position or Net Delta (e.g., October heating oil futures at $.0.44)

Option position	Delta	Net delta
Long 2 $0.44 calls	+ 0.52	+ 1.04
Long 3 $0.44 puts	− 0.49	− 1.47
Long 2 $0.46 calls	− 0.28	− 0.56
Total net delta	− 0.99	

Source: Kay (1988).

the-money deltas. Higher volatility increases the chance that out-of-the-money options will expire in the money, and vice versa.

Aside from its value in short-term trading, delta is a useful concept for the option hedger as well. By adding up option deltas, it is possible to construct an equivalent net futures position. The net delta measures the degree of hedge coverage afforded by a particular combination of option positions at any given moment. By adding or subtracting additional options to the original position and calculating their effect in terms of net futures equivalent, a hedger can continuously adjust risk/reward profiles in line with changing management objectives. In Table 8.3, a total of seven options have been combined to form the equivalent of one short futures position. These option positions would provide the same degree of price protection as would selling one futures contract. In most cases, this degree of price protection could better be gained by going into the futures market. However, options provide more flexibility when dynamic hedging, rather than complete price protection, is the objective.

PARTICIPANTS IN PETROLEUM OPTION TRADING

A market survey carried out in 1987 indicates that participants in crude oil options include eight integrated oil companies, four refiners, six trader-resellers, and twenty-five traders.

Like those in the futures markets, participants in option trading include hedgers and speculators, though the distinction between the two is not always easy. A hedger may use option trading to limit his losses in case prices move unfavorably. For example, a refiner who would need to buy 100,000 barrels of crude in two months may buy a call option at a desirable strike price. If the spot price moves above the strike price, he may exercise his option and purchase the crude through his option contract at the strike price. If the spot price drops below the strike price, he may buy his crude in the spot market, letting his option expire; he will, of course, lose the premium paid for the option.

Similarly, a trader with a long cash heating oil position (a trader who owns heating oil) can fix a minimum sale price by buying put options. If prices decline, the trader is hedged because he had already contracted the right to sell. If prices rally, the most the hedge will cost is the premium paid. Appreciation in the value of his inventory will offset some or all of the fixed costs of the hedge beyond which the trader can enjoy the benefit of higher selling prices in the spot market. Thus, the buy put strategy provides the trader downside protection without jeopardizing the trader's potential for profit when prices rally.

The hedging function is similar to the one carried out through a futures contract, with one major difference. In the case of the futures market, if the hedge works well (spot futures prices move together), the hedger will protect himself against the risk of unfavorable price movements, but he will also be forsaking the potential profit from favorable price movements. In the case of options, the hedger will protect himself against unfavorable price variations but still may benefit from unexpectedly favorable price movements. That is, he transfers the risk to the buying agent but still keeps some of the profit potential for himself. This is a more desirable hedging arrangement than the futures market can provide. The hedger, of course, pays a price—the option premium—for this more desirable hedging arrangement.

Hedging through options is also more flexible than hedging through the futures market. For example, the aforementioned refiner may want to take a hedging policy to limit losses only if the price movement is very unfavorable—say, a surge beyond $20.00/b due to some political event. He will then buy a call option with a strike price of $20.00/b, which would carry a small premium. The point is, with options, the hedger can choose the range of price he wants to avoid, and select the appropriate option or options, combination of futures, or combination of various options to achieve this goal. With options, a hedger can buy price insurance at a fixed cost (premium) to protect against adverse price movements without forgoing the potential to profit from favorable price movements. Further, he can choose the extent or coverage of the insurance and take the appropriate policy.

For speculators, option trading may provide an ideal tool. A speculator anticipating an increase in the price of oil may buy a call option. If the price does actually go up, he will profit as much as he would with a futures contract, minus the option premium. If the price drops, his loss will be limited to the premium paid for the option. A put option would serve a similar function for a speculator who anticipates a fall in the price. Frequently speculators limit their potential loss to even less than the option premium by combining options and futures or combining various options. As one moves toward more sophisticated methods and strategies, the management of the positions becomes more complicated, and premiums and transaction costs increase. It then becomes difficult to say who hedges and who speculates. What comes with this sophistication is flexibility and a wide range of methods to manage risk portfolios.

EXAMPLES OF HEDGING WITH PETROLEUM OPTIONS

In most hedging strategies, the hedge is designed to protect profits or asset values, or establish costs or revenues at favorable price levels.[10] The subsequent market action affects cash flow, not final costs. In a "fully hedged" approach, the objectives are set, the hedge ratio calculated, and the position implemented. Only when the cash transaction is executed is the offsetting hedge lifted. The use of futures permits the attainment of objectives not always available in the physical market, and the introduction of option strategies broadens considerably the range of goals achievable within either the physicals or futures markets.

To design an options-related strategy, three major issues must be considered and resolved:

• What is the objective of the risk manager (hedger)?
• What is the hedger's opinion or forecast for the related market during the hedging period?
• What has been the volatility of the underlying futures market, and what is it expected to be during the hedging term?

Based on these considerations, the hedging objectives will be set. On the producer side, these objectives may include:

• Locking in favorable prices for forward periods;

- Protecting the value of existing inventories or future production at current values;
- Setting a minimum price for future sales, yet participating if prices rise;
- Enhancing revenue by collecting a premium for accepting the obligation to sell a product above the current market price.

The first two objectives can be achieved using physicals or futures, but the last two require options techniques. On the consumer side, the objectives of hedging may include:

- Locking in favorable costs for forward periods;
- Protecting the value of raw materials purchased, goods-in-process, or finished goods at current values;
- Setting a maximum price for forward purchases, while benefiting if prices fall;
- Developing the potential to buy below the current market price and collecting a premium in so doing.

Again, the last two objectives incorporate option strategies rather than futures alone.

Although the use of futures strategies may not demand a market forecast, the choice of an appropriate options strategy requires some appraisal of likely market ranges over the hedge period. To illustrate:

- A strongly bullish forecast would suggest buying futures, buying calls, or writing (selling) puts.
- A strongly bearish forecast would suggest selling futures, buying puts, or writing (selling) calls.
- A moderately bullish strategy would suggest buying calls.
- An expectation of a narrow trading range with declining volatility might suggest writing both puts and calls.
- A directionless forecast with rising volatility might suggest buying puts and calls.

With the available futures and options instruments, one can design a wide range of hedging strategies. The following cases are a few examples of certain strategies that can be pursued on the production/distribution side, as well as on the consumption side.

An example of the use of options on the supply side is as follows. On October 1, a heating oil distributor has finalized a contract with a municipality to deliver heating oil at a guaranteed maximum price of $0.48 per gallon. The deliveries will occur in January 1989. If prices rise between October and January, the distributor, if unhedged, will be forced to absorb the higher costs. The distributor, however, may be reluctant to simply buy calls to protect against a rising market (a buyer of a call option has the right but not the obligation to buy futures at a specific price during the life of the option). Although the risk of a long call position is limited to its purchase price, this cost might seem excessive to the distributor should prices drop.

One strategy to reduce this initial cost is a three-part options spread designed to accommodate the distributor's forecast range of heating oil prices through the early winter. The approach calls for combining the buying and selling of February options at three different strike prices such that the net cost of the option spread is near zero. Specifically, the distributor could

- Sell a put at a strike price near the bottom of the expected trading range.
- Buy a call at a strike price near current futures price levels.
- Sell a call at a strike price near the top of the expected trading range.

It should be noted that the seller of a put expects the market not to fall below the strike price of the put option; the seller of a call expects the market not to trade above the strike price of the call option. If these forecasts prove valid, the seller of these options simply earns the premium originally collected.

The assumptions underlying the example are as follows:

- On October 1, February heating oil futures equal $0.47 per gallon.
- Distributor's market view: heating oil prices could fluctuate between $0.42 and $0.50 per gallon through early January.
- Heating oil cash and futures prices move in tandem.

The strategy is as follows:

- Buy February $0.48 call at $0.0200 per gallon.
- Sell February $0.50 call at $0.0135 per gallon.
- Sell February $0.42 put at $0.0065 per gallon.
  Net cost = zero

All options expire on January 13; option prices assume a volatility of 25 percent on October 1.

Table 8.4

Profit/Loss Outcome of a Heating Oil Hedge Program (per gallon)

No. 2 oil cash prices ($)	Physical sales price ($)	Gain or loss (physical) ($)	Gain or loss (short 42 put) ($)	Gain or loss (long 48 call) ($)	Gain or loss (short 50 call) ($)	Total profit (loss) ($)
0.40	0.48	0.08	(0.02)	–	–	0.06
0.42	0.48	0.06	–	–	–	0.06
0.44	0.48	0.04	–	–	–	0.04
0.46	0.48	–	–	–	–	0.02
0.48	0.48	–	–	–	–	0.00
0.50	0.48	(0.02)	–	0.02	–	0.00
0.50	0.48	(0.04)	–	0.04	(0.02)	(0.02)

Source: Kaplan and Beutel (1988).

Table 8.4 shows the profit/loss results of the hedge. It should be noted that with this hedge strategy, the distributor has significant flexibility. If the cash price falls, he has the ability to offer low prices to his customers, down to $0.42 per gallon without losing money on his hedge. Below $0.42, the short $0.42 put behaves like a long futures position, losing value tick for tick as heating oil prices fall. In this situation, the distributor will need to offset the loss on his hedge by maintaining his sales prices in the physical market.

If prices rally, the distributor will earn a profit on his long $0.48 call position up to $0.50 per gallon. Should prices continue to rally above $0.50 per gallon, the distributor's profit on his hedge is fixed, since the gain from the long $0.48 call will be offset by the loss from the $0.50 call. If the distributor believes, however, that $0.50 per gallon will be the maximum price during the winter, he is likely to realize full profit participation from the call spread.

An example of hedging on the demand side is as follows. An end user needs to hedge against possible increases in the price of heating oil by the time he will need to purchase and consume the oil. He can buy heating oil futures contracts at $0.45 per gallon. If he uses the futures market for hedging, a net price of $0.45 will be received regardless of how dramatically prices change. With options, however, he would have a different risk-reward profile (buy call strategies provide protection against an upward move in prices but allow participation in a downward price move). For example, the end user buys a December $0.46 call option for $0.0240 per gallon. The call option has established a maximum purchase price at $0.4840 per gallon, because the long call conveys the right to buy futures at $0.46 with a cost of $0.0240 ($0.4600 + 0.0240 = $0.4840). If prices rally above $0.46, the end user can exercise the call option. The flexibility of the long call strategy is illustrated when prices decline. If prices fall to $0.42 per gallon, the end user has a net purchase price of $0.4440 after accounting for the cost of the hedge ($0.0240). Because the cost of the hedge is fixed at $0.0240 (the premium), the end user is able to participate in market declines. Compared with the futures hedge, the buy call strategy is superior when prices decline. At $0.50, the futures hedge achieves a net purchase price of $0.4541, while the $0.46 call achieves a price of $0.4840. The futures hedge is superior if prices rally or if prices remain unchanged. If prices remain unchanged at $0.4541, the futures hedger pays $0.4541 for the oil; the options trader receives $0.4541 plus the premium paid ($0.0240), or $0.4781.

Trading different strike prices also alters the risk-reward profile of the hedger. For example, the $0.46 call establishes a $0.4840 ceiling, lower than the $0.4975 ceiling established by the $0.48 call, and lower than the $0.5125 maximum purchase price established by the $0.50 call. However, the best protection against an upside move costs the most. The premium for the $0.46 is $0.0240, while the $0.48 and $0.50 calls cost $0.0175 and $0.012, respectively. The cost of the option determines how much the hedger participates in a downward move in prices. With prices at $0.38 at expiration, the hedger who has purchased the $0.46 call pays a price of $0.4040, which is higher than the $0.3975 and the $0.3925 for the hedger who purchased the $0.48 or $0.50 call, respectively.

If an end user has the flexibility to withstand some increase in oil prices, a sell put strategy may be appropriate. By selling puts the oil company takes advantage of high premiums and expects sideways trading markets. The premium received from selling the puts acts a hedge against rising prices. Protection is, however, limited to the premium received. If prices decline, the company participates until prices reach the put's strike price. Losses on the short put then begin to offset gains on the cash position.

Net sales prices for three short put strategies are illustrated in Table 8.5. By selling $0.42 puts, the company buys heating oil for $0.0115 be-

Table 8.5
Hedging Results Using Futures and Options

| Futures at expiration ($) | Futures hedge | Net Purchase Price ($/gal) | | | | | | Fence B$46C S$44P |
| | | Buy calls | | | Sell puts | | | |
		$0.46	$0.48	$0.50	$0.44	$0.42	$0.40	
0.52	0.4541	0.4840	0.4975	0.5125	0.5010	0.5085	0.5130	0.4650
0.50	0.4541	0.4840	0.4975	0.5125	0.4810	0.4885	0.4930	0.4650
0.48	0.4541	0.4840	0.4975	0.4925	0.4610	0.4685	0.4730	0.4650
0.46	0.4541	0.4840	0.4775	0.4725	0.4410	0.4485	0.4530	0.4650
0.44	0.4541	0.4640	0.4575	0.4525	0.4210	0.4285	0.4330	0.4450
0.42	0.4541	0.4440	0.4375	0.4325	0.4210	0.4085	0.4130	0.4450
0.40	0.4541	0.4240	0.4175	0.4125	0.4210	0.4085	0.3930	0.4450
0.38	0.4541	0.4040	0.3975	0.3925	0.4210	0.4085	0.3930	0.4450
Net debit	(0.0240)	(0.0175)	(0.0125)		(0.0050)			
Net credit			0.0190	0.0115	0.0070			

Source: Colburn (1988).

low the market price if prices remain above $0.42. Otherwise, if prices move lower, the hedger pays $0.4085, or the strike price minus the premium. Selling $0.42 puts against a short cash position brings in less cash than the short $0.40 put strategy. This implies that the $0.40 put is not as effective as a hedge against higher prices as is the $0.42 put. The tradeoff is that the short $0.40 call allows for more participation if prices move lower. The lowest price at which the hedger can buy heating oil using the $0.40 strategy is $0.3930, which is $0.0055 lower than if the $0.42 short put hedge strategy had been chosen. Selling the $0.40 call takes in the least amount of premium but allows for the most downside participation of the three sell put strategies.

A hedger may like the idea of establishing a floor or ceiling price through buy call strategies but may feel that premiums are too expensive. The hedger could sell out-of-the-money puts and use the premium received to offset the cost of the calls. This strategy is called a "collar" or a "fence." In the example, the hedger sells $0.44 puts to offset the cost of buying $0.46 calls. The puts are sold for $0.0190 and the calls are bought for $0.0240, a net debit of $0.0050 per gallon. The maximum purchase price is established at $0.4650. If prices rise above $0.46, the hedger exercises the option to buy at $0.46 and has paid the $0.0050 premium up front.

Reducing the cash cost of a call by selling a put is not done without some tradeoff. In this case, the hedger is giving up any downside participation below $0.44. If prices go below $0.44, gains made on the short cash position are offset by losses on the short put position. For example, at $0.38, the hedger buys heating oil for $0.38 but loses $0.06 on the short $0.46 put. The hedger paid $0.0050 up front, so the net purchase price is $0.4450.

Fences are effective hedging strategies for oil companies that need to establish maximum purchase prices and yet would like to participate in a down market. Floors and ceilings can be adjusted to reflect the amount of downside protection needed, the level of upside participation, and the amount of cash paid or received up front. The fence allows the hedger to remove extreme volatility in price movements at low cost.

VOLUME OF OPTION TRADING

NYMEX crude oil options have become the second most actively traded commodity option, trailing only the Treasury bond option contract traded on the Chicago Board of Trade. The trading volume of crude oil options averaged 10,000 contracts per day in 1987. By the second half of the year, the trading volume increased to over 15,000 contracts a day, and on August 20, it hit a record high of 44,992 contracts. The daily number of contracts was in the range of 20,000 to 25,000 from 1988 to 1990.

Acceptance of crude oil options by the oil industry has been quite rapid. In contrast to petroleum futures contracts, which after their introduction took some time to be taken seriously by the oil industry, options trading grew rapidly shortly after its introduction. There are at least two major reasons behind this rapid growth. First, extensive volatility of petroleum prices in 1986-87 has provided the right condition for options trading. In particular, many hedging positions on the futures market have now turned into a combination of futures and option contracts. Second, options trading was not introduced until after the oil industry had a relatively long period to digest petroleum futures. When options arrived, the petroleum industry was already active in the futures market and viewed the option contract as simply one more instrument of risk management.

Heating oil options have grown at a much slower pace. The average volume was about 1,400 contracts per day in 1990. The unleaded gasoline option has done slightly better, with a trading volume of about 2,000 contracts per day in 1990.

PART FOUR

The Market
Interlinkages

CHAPTER 9

The Impact of Futures Trading on Petroleum Stock Movements

Oil stocking is not a new phenomenon. Historically, the petroleum industry has carried operating stocks to maintain the smooth functioning of its production and distribution systems. These stocks were, until a decade ago, a matter of small concern. They were viewed as a technically necessary element of the industry's operation, with no significant impact on the level or pattern of petroleum prices. The structural changes of the oil industry in the 1970s have, however, changed the role and the importance of petroleum stocks in the oil market. The panic inventory buildup of 1979 contributed significantly to the rapid increase in the price of crude oil. On the other hand, the worldwide excess supply of crude oil in 1981–82 and 1986–87 was exacerbated by the destocking of crude oil inventories, which were then released due to the anticipation of a decline in the price of oil.

Despite their traditional stabilizing role, petroleum inventories now have the potential to destabilize the market. The management of oil stocks is increasingly based on speculation about their future price. At present, a considerable portion of inventory variations represents so-called speculative stock movement. This type of stock movement is a direct response to the fluctuation in the price of oil and to the increasing importance of the spot market as a supplement to traditional means of oil trading. The movement of speculative stock is triggered only by the expectation of making a profit through a change in the price. This type of stock is accumulated during a period when a price increase is anticipated and is released once the expectation of a price rise fades away. Unlike operational stocks, which follow a well-defined pattern and have the aim of stabilizing and smoothing out market fluctuations, speculative stock has a distorting impact on the supply and demand relationship and enhances market imbalances. That is, speculative demand for oil exerts upward pressure on prices during a shortage and downward pressure during a period of oversupply.

Speculative stockpiling and futures trading interact in several ways:

- To the extent that this type of stockpiling destabilizes the spot market price, futures trading will increase to take advantage of the resultant price volatility.
- The futures market may itself affect the stability of the spot market price and thereby change the prospects for speculative stockpiling.
- Futures trading may partially substitute for speculative stock movements.

In this chapter, the interactions between petroleum stock movements and oil futures trading are analyzed. First, a description of various types of petroleum stocks is presented. A discussion of the motivations of the agents involved in building these stocks follows. Finally, the potential reactions of each type of stock and stockpiler to the emergence of futures trading in the petroleum business are assessed.

VARIOUS TYPES OF PETROLEUM STOCKS

Petroleum stocks may be classified into three broad categories: (a) operating stocks, (b) strategic and mandatory stocks, and (c) speculative stocks.

Operating Stocks

Operating stocks are held by the petroleum industry to keep the production and distribution systems on course. A major portion of the operating stock is used to keep the oil logistical system functioning. This includes the filling of tankers, pipelines, and tank cars with crude oil being moved from producing fields to storage terminals, crude transported from terminals to refiners, oil being processed, and the enormous amount of refined products flowing in the distribution network.

Another portion of the operating stock is used to provide a precautionary[11] buffer against "normal" interruptions in supplies or pro-

Exhibit 9.1
Petroleum Stocks by Type and Sector

―――――――――――――――――――――――――――――――――――

Various types of stocks

- Operating stocks, including:

  (1) oil flowing in the production and distribution systems;

  (2) precautionary stocks; and

  (3) seasonal stocks.

- Strategic and mandatory stocks, including:

  (1) strategic reserves;

  (2) minimum stock levels; and

  (3) public corporations' emergency reserves.

- Speculative stocks maintained by all sectors of the petroleum industry.

Where the stocks are held

- Primary stocks, including:

  (1) crude oil stored at producing fields;

  (2) stocks at tanker loading ports;

  (3) crude and products at sea and in pipelines;

  (4) crude and products at discharge terminals;

  (5) crude and products at refineries; and

  (6) refined products at large distribution terminals.

- Secondary stocks, including:

  (1) stocks held by small distribution stations;

  (2) inventories held by wholesalers and marketers; and

  (3) inventories held by retailers and gas stations.

- Tertiary stocks, including:

  (1) gasoline in automobile tanks;

  (2) heating oil in residential storage;

  (3) fuel oil inventories held by power utilities; and

  (4) product inventories held by industrial users.

―――――――――――――――――――――――――――――――――――

duction activity. Such interruptions include normal maintenance, seasonal retrofitting related to product mix variations, and "normal" accidents.

Finally, an important function of operating stock is to facilitate customer transactions. The industry uses part of the operating stock to manage an efficient production process as consumption of petroleum products undergoes seasonal and/or cyclical variations. For example, heating oil produced in summer is stocked for its peak use in winter, and motor gasoline produced in winter is stocked for its peak use in summer.

Strategic and Mandatory Stocks

Strategic and mandatory stocks are maintained in many countries to reduce the impact of disruptions in petroleum supplies. They are under direct or indirect control of the governments of these countries. Governments may take some or all of the following measures:

- The establishment of a strategic petroleum reserve (SPR);
- The imposition of minimum mandatory stock levels that must be held by the private oil sector;
- The formation of public corporations that finance and manage the emergency reserve program.

At present, about twenty countries have chosen to implement one or two of the above programs, while West Germany is involved in all three. The United States has implemented only one program, the strategic reserve, which is directly owned and controlled by the U.S. government. This program was created by the Energy Policy and Conservation Act of 1975. The program calls for the construction and filling of a one-billion-barrel reserve of crude oil and/or petroleum products. Japan and Sweden have also decided to build strategic petroleum reserves. However, both Japan and Sweden are instituting their programs in conjunction with the minimum mandatory stocks held by the private sector. Denmark, the Netherlands, and Switzerland have established public corporations which are financed and managed by the government to build emergency reserves. All other Organisation of Economic Co-operation and Development (OECD) countries, except Canada and New Zealand, have decided to implement a mandatory reserve program that will be held by private companies. Many private companies resent this program because of the financial burden it imposes. High interest rates and the fluctuating prices of petroleum products contribute to this burden.

Speculative Stocks

Speculative stocks emerged as the result of fluctuations in the price of oil, the tendency of contracts to become increasingly short term, and speculators' accessibility to oil supplies through the spot market. The main objective of this type of stockpiling is to maximize the expected profit, or minimize the losses, from holding the stock during a period of price adjustment. Therefore, the basic determinants in decisions to stockpile are the expected increase or decrease in the price of oil, and the cost associated with keeping the stock for a certain period. The key to the analysis of speculative stockpiling is to provide a realistic configuration of these determinants.

The expected change in the price of oil is normally related to the difference between the supply of and demand for oil. Though such a relationship can serve as a useful tool for the assessment of long-term price movements, it provides little insight into the short-term price fluctuations that are of concern to the speculative stockpiler. Short-term speculation about changes in the price of oil is normally based on OPEC's capacity utilization factor, despite the fact that OPEC has become a residual energy supplier.

From the stockpiler's point of view, there are three distinct phases of capacity utilization, each having its own implications with regard to future prices. The main determinant of these phases is the OPEC member countries' production capacity, which may vary over time. It is usually assumed that OPEC member countries have a desire to operate at their "normal" capacity. This is not the maximum or normal physical capacity, but the level of operation that fits the member countries' overall politico-economic strategies. If market forces are pressuring OPEC member countries to operate above normal capacity, then the expectation of a price increase is likely to grow in the market. The expected rate of the price rise is itself an increasing function of such market pressures. Clearly, any unexpected disruption in the oil production of one or a few member countries will sharply decrease available capacity and, at the same time, increase the capacity utilization rate in other countries. This disruption creates the expectation of a price rise.

Below normal capacity utilization, there is a range of operations that is considered tolerable by member countries. Within this range, OPEC is not expected to change its price. The decline of the capacity utilization rate to a level that cannot be tolerated by some or all OPEC members will, however, lead to speculation of a fall in oil prices. Here again, the expected rate of the price fall will itself increase as the capacity utilization factor declines further.

HOLDERS OF THE STOCKS

Oil inventories are held at various stages of the worldwide distribution network in the form of crude oil, refinery feedstocks, blending components, and finished products. Although distribution and storage systems vary among countries, petroleum inventories are generally classified into three categories:

- Primary
- Secondary
- Tertiary

This classification corresponds to the structure of the petroleum distribution system. That is, the system itself is composed of three sectors—primary, secondary, and tertiary—and the petroleum stock held in each sector is named accordingly.

Primary

The primary sector gathers crude oil, transports it to refineries, processes it into products, and delivers those products in bulk to the secondary distribution system. The petroleum stocks held in this sector include crude oil stored at producing fields, stocks at tanker loading ports, crude oil and products at sea and in pipeline, crude oil and products at discharge terminals, crude oil and products at refineries, and refined products at large distribution terminals.

Secondary

The secondary sector of the distribution system begins at the point at which products leave the primary sector via tank truck, rail, or barge for small distribution stations closer to the market, and ends where products are received by consumers. The inventories in this sector are held by small distribution stations, retailers, wholesalers, marketers, and gas stations.

Tertiary

The tertiary inventories refer to the stocks held by end users. These inventories constitute a major portion of petroleum stocks and include gasoline in automobile tanks, heating oil in residential storages, residual and distillate fuel oil stocks at utilities, and fuel oil stocks in storage for industrial use.

THE LEVEL OF PETROLEUM STOCKS

Statistics on petroleum stocks are very abstract: with regard to the types of stocks, there is no information on how much of the stock movement is related to the operational needs of the industry and what portion is due to speculative incentives; with regard to the holders of stocks, all reported statistics are available only on the inventories of the primary sector. Secondary and tertiary inventories are normally omitted from the industry's reporting system, since collecting and disseminating the data of these inventories would be extremely expensive. Once oil gets into the distribution and consumption channels, it is virtually lost to statisticians. Even within the primary sector, only 75 percent of the world's inventory is reported by official sources (in Europe, the United States, and Japan). Estimates of the remaining 25 percent are normally based on industrial activity, etc. Thus, statistics on world oil inventories are inherently imprecise. Indeed, they are more an assessment than actual data.

No one knows how large the secondary and tertiary, and thus, total world inventories are. Some industry experts estimate that the total oil contained within the distribution chain is about 10 billion barrels. Of this amount, approximately 4.8 billion barrels are held in the primary sector, and the remaining 5.2 billion barrels are in the secondary and tertiary sectors.

Figure 9.1 shows the quarterly time series of U.S. petroleum stocks during the period 1965–87. In early 1978, the industry found itself caught with high stocks. It then began to release the stock in order to avoid the capital loss associated with a price decline. When stocks bottomed out and demand increased in late 1978, the industry faced the subsequent period of crude oil price increases with low stocks. The low initial stocks and the demand for speculative stocks in 1979 acted to push the price of oil even higher than it would have reached due to the

Figure 9.1
Quarterly Series of U.S. Oil Stocks

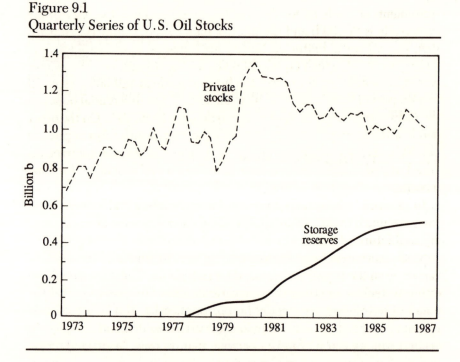

supply interruptions after the Iranian revolution. Despite the increasing price of oil in 1979, the industry added 29 million barrels to its stock. Conversely, in 1981 and 1982, the U.S. petroleum industry reduced its level of stock by 17 million and 13 million barrels, respectively, despite a declining oil price. In short, the stock buildup and withdrawal decisions of the petroleum industry have become, by and large, speculative in the sense that they are very dependent on the industry's expectation of future prices.

INTERACTIONS BETWEEN PETROLEUM STOCKPILING AND OIL FUTURES TRADING

From a theoretical point of view it can be shown that a producer would utilize the futures market versus storing a commodity to the point that he equates the "marginal carrying cost" of the inventory with the futures price net of the spot price. For example, if the carrying cost of crude oil is $0.10/b per month and a refiner needs to secure his requirements of crude oil for the next four months, and if the price of the spot crude is $19.00/b and the price of four-month futures is $20.00/b, then the refiner is better off buying his crude oil now, storing it, and paying 4 x $0.10, which equals $0.40/b, for the storage fee. The refiner would, of course, prefer to buy the futures crude at $20.00/b. Since all market participants make a similar calculation, the differential between the futures price and the spot price would drop to $0.40/b. On the other hand, if the spot price is $19.00/b and the four-month futures price is $19.20/b, then the refiner is better off buying the futures contract instead of purchasing the oil now at $15.00/b and storing it for four months.

In practice, interactions between futures trading and storage decisions are much more complicated, due to uncertainties in demand, supply, and future prices.

Stock movements and futures trading are, in general, responses to variations in the supply and demand for petroleum. These variations are either systematic or random. Systematic variations in the supply and demand of petroleum are, by definition, predictable and lead to movements of operating stocks. Random variations in demand and supply generate an opportunity for speculation that, in turn, leads to speculative stock movements as well as to futures trading.

Random variations are due to several factors. Almost all forces affecting the supply and demand of petroleum involve some uncertain elements. On the demand side, there are considerable uncertainties in the prediction of business cycles, seasonal factors, conservation, and substitution, as well as institutional matters such as natural gas deregulation, etc. Random variations on the demand side, however, are relatively small (compared with the supply side) because demand does not undergo sharp changes, and the behavior of demand is better understood.

Random variations in supply are the result of uncertainties in predicting the politico-economic conditions of oil-producing countries as well as institutional factors such as the OPEC coalition. Random variations on the supply side are relatively large for two reasons: the policy environment of oil-producing countries can undergo sharp changes over a short period of time, and supply behavior is not yet well understood.

Regardless of the source, uncertainties exist and lead to speculative activities in the oil market. These activities were, until the early 1980s, confined to speculative stockpiling. However, since 1983–84, petroleum futures markets have significantly changed speculative stockpiling decisions. These futures have, indeed, affected the stockpiling decisions of the petroleum industry in all sectors of the distribution system.

OIL FUTURES AS A SUBSTITUTE FOR PETROLEUM STOCKS

Petroleum futures can partially substitute for speculative stocks. They can also be utilized to manage the operating inventory more effectively but cannot substitute for the strategic reserves.

Operating stocks are often perceived to depend solely on levels of production and consumption. This perception is not completely warranted. It is true that these stocks are necessary to facilitate the production and distribution of petroleum products. However, any type of facility has its own price, and its demand declines as the price increases. Even the "minimum" operating stock varies as economic conditions change. When the cost of holding inventory increases, all elements of the petroleum distribution network attempt to use operating stocks more efficiently. In particular, since 1978, higher oil prices and interest rate levels have made the cost of holding inventory very high. The estimated cost of holding one gallon of gasoline inventory in 1978 was about $0.04 per year. In 1981 it soared to $0.19; since then it has stabilized around $0.10 per year.

Thus, many firms in the petroleum industry try to manage their inventories so that no more than the required levels are held. Petroleum futures provide a tool that can be used by refiners to make more efficient use of their operating stock. For example, a significant portion of operating stock is held to cope with seasonal variations of the product mix demand. A refiner who is stockpiling gasoil for winter's peak demand may be concerned with a possible decline in the level of petroleum prices. He can use the futures market to hedge against the price decline and manage his inventory based on his customers' demand. Or, if a refiner is concerned with the relative price movements of his operating crude and refined inventories, he can take two opposite positions in crude oil and products futures to lock in the price margin and then manage the inventories based on the production and distribution requirements.

Strategic petroleum reserves and futures trading have one trait in common. They both respond to an interruption in the supply of petroleum, but they respond, however, in completely different ways. If such a disruption occurs, the government will release strategic reserves to prevent a drastic jump in the level of oil prices (and its consequential impact on the allocation of resources). Thus, strategic reserves function as a source of petroleum supply during the period of disruption. Futures trading, however, does not provide a source of supply under such circumstances. It merely reflects the prevailing shortage in the form of soaring futures prices. Therefore, futures markets cannot provide a substitute for strategic reserves. Indeed, it can be argued that, with the presence of futures markets, the need for and the complexity of managing strategic reserves become quite severe. With futures markets serving as the main channel of the industry's immediate reaction to political events, the market price will respond to the news of a disruption in a matter of seconds and with an exaggerated magnitude. The strategic reserve can dampen the price hike only if it is released in a timely manner and in a sufficient amount.

Speculative stockpiling and futures trading emerge from the same source and are undertaken for the same incentive. They both exist when the price is volatile and are both based on speculation and/or hedging motivations. Speculative stocks are held in all three (primary, secondary, and tertiary) sectors of the distribution system. When a price increase is anticipated, all stocks, from crude oil lease tanks to refinery inventories and end-user storage, tend to go up. All stockholders are motivated to keep a higher level of inventory to profit from, or hedge against, a price rise.

Futures trading provides a convenient substitute for many speculative movements of petroleum stocks. An independent refiner who builds a stock of crude oil to hedge against a rise in the price of crude may buy crude oil futures instead. A major oil company that maintains an inventory of heating oil throughout the year to meet its customer demand does not need to lower its level of inventory to reduce the loss associated with a possible decline in petroleum prices. Instead, it can sell futures contracts and avoid the risk. A marketer who wants to make a forward commitment to his customer and is not able to obtain a price commitment from the supplier does not need to increase his inventory in order to avoid the loss associated with a price rise. He can buy a futures contract and safely commit forward sales to his customers at fixed prices. Finally, industrial and commercial customers of petroleum products who fill up their storage in order to avoid the risk of a price rise, or lower their storage to an inconvenient level to avoid the risk associated with a price fall, can instead use the futures market for the purpose of risk aversion while at the same time maintaining a normal inventory level for the smooth functioning of their operation.

Petroleum futures have affected the industry's stockpiling decisions, but their impact is likely to become even more substantial in the future. A survey of NYMEX participants in 1987 shows that five of the six major international oil companies rank among the main players in the futures market, accounting for 25 percent of the total trade. Refiners and marketers each make up 15 percent of the trade. The remaining 45 percent is distributed among traders including investment banking houses. The refiners' and marketers' futures trading decisions are closely related to their stockpiling policies. However, the majors do not necessarily use the market in conjunction with their stockpiling decisions. One group that is not yet fully involved is the end users of petroleum products. Most end users are able to pass the cost of their fuel to the consumers of their final products. Thus, end users do not have a strong incentive to become involved in the complicated business of avoiding the risk of a rise in the price of their fuels. Also, most of the end users are concerned with the physical supply of petroleum. Thus, they prefer to buy the "wet barrels" of oil and to buy them from "oilmen" rather than from commodity traders in the futures market. Nevertheless, large consumers have begun to utilize the futures market mostly to hedge against undesirable price movements.

CONCLUSION

Petroleum stockpiling is one part of the oil industry that has been significantly affected by futures trading. Of the various types of stockpiling, speculative stocking of petroleum interacts most intensively with the oil futures market. Holders of speculative inventories, and thus the potential users of futures markets, are scattered in all three (primary, secondary, and tertiary) sectors of the petroleum distribution system. However, at present, most of the petroleum stockpilers involved in the futures market are from the secondary sector. Stockpilers in the primary sector are not yet using the futures market extensively in conjunction with inventory decisions. Stockpilers in the tertiary sector are even less involved but are likely to increase their involvement as the cost-effectiveness of obtaining energy resources becomes as important as the security of physical supply.

CHAPTER 10

Interactions Between Futures Trading and the Spot Market Price

BEHAVIOR OF FUTURES PRICES

Futures markets are sometimes believed to destabilize the spot market in order to provide speculative opportunities. This perception is not, in general, correct. Futures trading can actually help the spot market work more effectively.

In the absence of a futures market, the spot market provides guidelines for the producers to organize and distribute their supplies. In addition, the spot market serves as a means of sharing risk among some producing and consuming agents. If a trader wants to avoid the risk on the value of his inventory, he will sell part of his inventory in the spot market. Consequently, some other agent in the industry will assume the risk through the spot market mechanism. The spot market will then have a dual function to serve—that is, the provision of supply and demand guidelines *and* the sharing of risk. However, it cannot serve either function in the most effective manner, because no organ can satisfy a dual objective as efficiently as it can a single one. If a futures market is introduced and can play its role effectively, then the second function of the spot market—risk sharing—is transferred to the futures market.

Therefore, the spot market can play its primary function—facilitating the interaction of supply and demand forces—more efficiently.

When futures trading exists in a market, speculators find it more convenient to deal in futures contracts than to buy a quantity of the commodity at the current spot price and hold it with the hope that there will be a rise in the spot price. In the same manner, traders who want to avoid the risk of a price decline can do so more conveniently by selling futures contracts than by selling the commodity in the spot market. Thus, the risk-sharing function of the spot market is transferred to the futures market.

Although the futures and the spot market will serve, at least theoretically, two distinct functions, the interaction between the two markets constitutes the most important aspect of futures trading. This interaction is normally studied by exploring the relationship between spot and futures prices.

There are two important factors to consider in this relationship:

- The relationship between the futures prices and the forthcoming spot market price (the spot price that will prevail in the delivery month)[12]
- The relationship between futures contract prices and the current spot market price (the cash market price)

With regard to the first factor, most studies have concluded that there is no significant correlation between the two prices. The conclusion denies one of the important functions—providing information about future price trends—that many analysts have attributed to futures trading. The empirical evidence has shown that the correlation between futures prices and the spot price in the delivery period is very weak. The lack of a strong correlation has been intuitively explained by the idea that any information about future supply-and-demand conditions that becomes available is incorporated in the current spot market price. Thus, there is no reason for futures contract prices to contain more information about future market conditions than the current spot price.[13] Figure 10.1 shows an example of the correlation between the two-month futures price of crude oil contracts and the spot price at their maturity date. The pattern observed in this period indicates that futures prices are not good estimators of the spot price at the maturity date.

With regard to the second factor—the relationship between futures contract prices and current spot prices—most studies have found a very strong correlation between the two. An example of this strong correlation is shown in Figure 10.2, which plots the price in a typical period

Figure 10.1
Crude Oil Two-Month Futures Prices and the Spot Price at Maturity
Date Traded on NYMEX in a Typical Period (West Texas Intermediate)

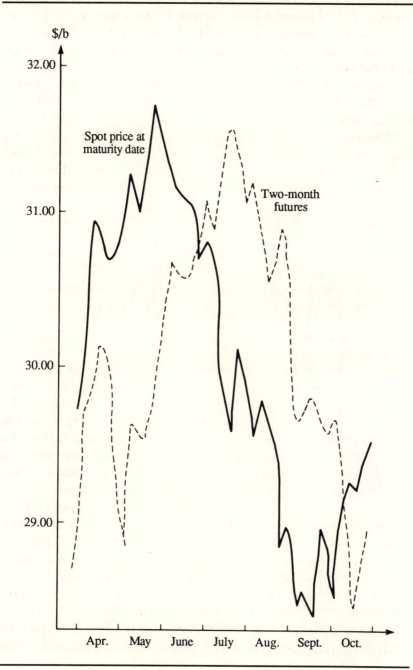

Source: Compiled from data provided by the New York Mercantile Exchange

Figure 10.2
Spot, Two-Month, and Five-Month Futures Prices of Crude Oil
Traded on NYMEX in a Typical Period (West Texas Intermediate)

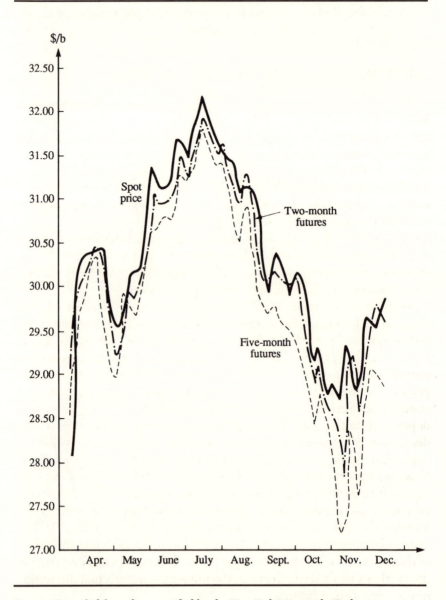

Source: Compiled from data provided by the New York Mercantile Exchange

(1983) of two-month and five-month crude oil futures, along with their cash market price. Is, however, the futures price affecting or simply following the spot market price? This is, of course, a critical determinant of the impact of oil futures trading on the structure of the petroleum market. A detailed discussion of this issue awaits presentation of the essentials of futures contract pricing below.

THE LIMITS TO PREMIUMS AND DISCOUNTS

The examples of hedging in previous chapters were simplified to illustrate the major points of the process. The complexities involved in actual transactions were omitted. In the real world, however, a hedge may not provide complete protection against undesired price movements. In the previous examples of hedging, it was assumed that spot and futures prices would rise and fall by exactly the same amount. There certainly is a tendency for spot and futures prices to move up and down together because the two markets must sell at the same price during the delivery period. Spot prices can, however, change a little faster or slower than futures prices. The difference between spot and futures prices, therefore, will change over time. This is especially true for the difference between the spot and the more distant futures.

Suppose, for example, that there is a disruption in the oil supply due to a political event in the Middle East. The immediate reaction of the petroleum market will appear in the form of higher spot prices. In the futures markets, two distinct effects would occur. First, the price of the current month's contracts will rise by almost the same amount as spot prices, because a current month's contract is equivalent to a spot market transaction. Second, more distant futures will be affected differently depending on the expected length of the disruption. If traders expect disruption of a temporary nature, then distant futures prices will not appreciate by as much as the near futures and spot prices. Conversely, if the disruption appears to be of a long-term nature, then prices of the distant futures will go up by as much as the spot and near futures prices. In a more usual case—that is, when the disruption is of an uncertain length—the spot price and the near futures price rise significantly. The prices of more distant futures will also go up considerably, but the extent of this increase will be less than the rise in the spot price. This is due to the market's tendency to discount the impact of an uncertain disruption into a more distant future.

Under both normal and abnormal circumstances, the various future months do not sell at the same price. Rather, they are sold at premiums or at discounts to each other. They are also sold at premiums or discounts to spot market prices.

In general, there are no specific rules for determining the amount of premiums or discounts. The reason why these premiums or discounts exist is, however, clear. A premium prevails in instances in which a commodity is valued more highly in the future than in the present. There is an upper limit to this premium. The maximum value is the marginal cost of holding a unit of the physical commodity from the present date until the maturity of the futures contract. This is due to the stockholder's having the option of keeping the unit in inventory and selling it in a future month. The marginal cost of holding a unit of stock consists of the physical storage cost, interest on the capital employed to hold the storage, insurance, and delivery cost.

The premium can be less than the maximum amount described above. Present inventory is often preferred over future stocks. The availability of an inventory to meet unforeseen demand offers a "convenience yield" or "accessibility benefit." This benefit is weighed against the carrying cost of inventory. If the benefit is less than the cost, there will be a positive premium that will stay between zero and the marginal carrying cost. If the benefit is more than the cost, however, an "inverted market" exists in which futures contracts are sold at a discount to spot prices. Since there is no limit to the convenience benefit, there is no ceiling to the discount. Thus, the premium is subject to an upper limit, but the discount is not bound to vary within a definite range. Nevertheless, premiums and discounts are both based on the same concept and both measure the same variable (normally called the "basis") in a positive and negative direction, respectively.

The "basis" (premium or discount) depends on the level of available inventory compared with the current and future prospects for sales (supply and demand conditions). As the level of inventory increases, the convenience yield tends to decline. At the same time, when the level of inventory increases, the carrying costs are likely to rise. Thus, at high levels of inventory, the basis tends to be positive and relatively large. Conversely, at lower levels of inventory, the convenience yield becomes quite significant, imparting a high value to the present inventory, and increasing the likelihood of a negative basis.

The term *basis*, as used in the trading community, has in general a broader definition than discussed above. It is normally used to refer to three types of price differentials:

• Intertemporal (time) price differences for an identical good

Exhibit 10.1
Basis (Premium or Discount) in the Futures Market

Intertemporal Basis

- Refers to the premium or the discount between contracts of various months (contracts with various maturity dates).
- The premium or discount of distant futures to the current month's futures depends on the convenience benefit from holding an inventory versus the cost of holding that inventory.
- Premium has a limit.
- Discount has no limit.

Quality Basis

- Refers to the premium or the discount of any quality to the *par* quality (determined in the contract).

Spatial Basis

- Refers to the premium or the discount of any delivery location to the standard location (determined in the contract).

- Grade (quality) price differentials
- Spatial (location) price differentials

The intertemporal basis depends (as discussed previously) on the convenience yield and the carrying cost of inventory. Grade price differentials are related to the variation in quality of the commodity. For example, the par quality for crude oil futures contracts at NYMEX is specified to contain 0.4 percent sulphur. If the sulphur content is different from this amount, there will be a \$0.05/b premium over the contract price for each 0.1 percent sulphur content less than par. In the same manner, there will be a \$0.05/b discount under the contract price for each 0.1 percent sulphur content greater than par. That is, there is a grade basis equal to \$0.05/b between two crudes with a 0.1 percent difference in sulphur content.

Spatial price differentials represent the price variation in various delivery locations. Again, as an example, the par crude in the IPE contract is deliverable in Rotterdam/Amsterdam, but other locations may be used at agreed discounts and premiums.

Figure 10.3 shows the intertemporal basis for crude oil for a typical period (1983). Empirical studies on other "continuously storable com-

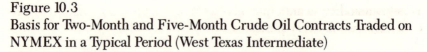

Figure 10.3

Basis for Two-Month and Five-Month Crude Oil Contracts Traded on NYMEX in a Typical Period (West Texas Intermediate)

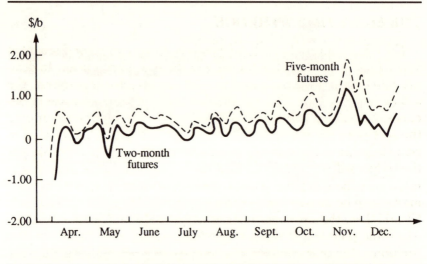

Source: Compiled from data provided by the New York Mercantile Exchange

modities" have shown that spot and futures prices often move in a parallel fashion. Thus, the basis remains relatively stable over time. As Figure 10.3 shows, the case of the crude oil market is no exception. The basis has remained relatively stable during the entire year.

A concept related to the above discussion is the "spread." A spread is the difference between the prices of two futures contracts of the same commodity but with two different maturity dates. This difference is normally adjusted to take account of the span between the times of delivery in order to make spreads comparable. More specifically, a spread is the amount in cents per barrel (gallon or tonne) per month someone would earn if he were to buy a contract, take delivery when the contract matures, and hold the oil to deliver on the forthcoming contract that he had sold.

In futures market language, the position in a futures market that earns the spread between the prices for different months of delivery is itself referred to as a spread. For example, the purchase of an October contract at the same time as the sale of a December contract is called a spread. A synonym for this meaning of spread is the term *straddle*. This term refers to buying one delivery position and selling another in the same commodity, in anticipation of a change in the price differential between the two delivery positions.

THE RIGHT TIME TO HEDGE

The effectiveness of a hedge depends on the premium or discount at which futures contracts are traded over the spot market price. In dealing with futures contracts traded at a full carrying charge premium, the selling hedge will be effective whether the spot price advances or declines. The hedger will sell the futures contract at a high premium over the spot price. At the same time, the spot and futures prices tend to come together as the maturity date for futures approaches. This means the hedger will be able to buy back the futures contract at a lower premium over the spot price. That is, the hedger's gain (loss) in the futures market will be greater (smaller) than his loss (gain) in the spot market. Clearly then, the advantage of a selling hedge depends on the extent to which the premium is closer to the full carrying cost. The lower this premium, the less will be the advantage of a selling hedge. In this sense, the carrying cost establishes a benchmark (a ceiling to the premium) that can be utilized to appraise the desirability of the conditions for a selling hedge.

The situation for a buying hedge is the opposite to that of a selling hedge. More specifically, when futures contracts are traded at a full carrying cost premium over the spot price, the buying hedge is not likely to be very successful. In fact, the buying hedge may, in such a case, lead to losses greater than if no hedge were utilized. (This may happen if the basis risk is greater than the commodity's cash market price variations.) The futures contract should, in general, be sold when its premium over the spot price is high and bought when the premium is low. (This is again due to the fact that as the maturity of a futures contract approaches, the spot price and the futures price tend to come together.)

Hedging in inverted market conditions (a market is "inverted" when futures prices are lower than the spot price) is a totally different matter. Under such market conditions, a futures contract is sold at a discount to the spot market price. The extent of this discount, as explained previously, does not have a limit. So there is no benchmark for comparison or basis to judge the desirability of the hedge. Under such circumstances, the advantage of the hedge should be evaluated based on the analysis of market prospects.

In an inverted market, futures prices are normally stronger and more stable than the spot market price: this is due, as mentioned above, to

Figure 10.4
Hedging in an Inverted Market

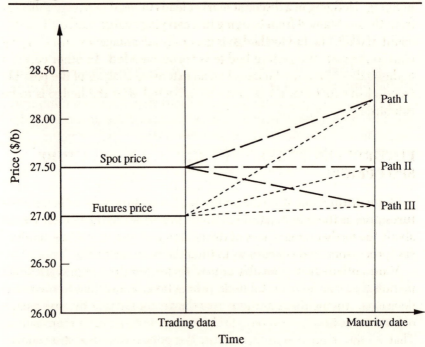

the fact that futures prices are already lower than the spot market price.
When the futures contract approaches its maturity, its price has to come
close to the spot price. By that time, the hedger may find himself in one
of the following three situations:

- The spot market price has remained constant, in which case the futures price
  should rise to approach the spot market price (Path II in Figure 10.4).
- The spot market price has increased, in which case the futures price has to
  increase faster to reach the spot price (Path I in Figure 10.4).
- The spot market price has declined, in which case the futures price will decline by a smaller amount to equal the spot price at the maturity date (Path
  III in Figure 10.4).

Thus, in an inverted market, the buying hedge is likely to be effective,
whereas a selling hedge may only be partially effective or even ineffec-
tive as a means of price protection.

In short, the relationship between the spot price and the futures price is the principal determinant of the advantages and disadvantages of hedging. Hedging in a discount market leads to results that are different from those obtained from hedging in a carrying charge market. In a discount market, the buying hedge is generally advantageous; in a carrying charge market, the selling hedge is recommended. In other cases, a hedging decision must be based on an extensive analysis of the possible trend of the spot market price to be expected after the hedge is to be established.

FUTURES PRICES AND THE PREDICTION OF FUTURE SPOT PRICES

Quite distinct but still related to the above discussion of the spot/futures price is the role that futures trading plays in providing information about the forthcoming prices of the commodity and in guiding producers, processors, and consumers in their decision-making.

Many authors have plausibly argued that futures prices provide information that can be used to guide production, storage, and processing decisions. Among these authors, some have argued that the emergence of futures trading is a response to the economic demand for information. That is, the main role of futures trading is to collect and disseminate information about future spot prices.

The efficiency of futures prices as estimators of forthcoming spot prices depends on the closeness between the two prices and the confidence attached to the expected price difference (between futures and forthcoming spot prices). The greater the efficiency with which futures prices serve as estimators of forthcoming spot prices, the better is the quality of information imparted by futures trading. Several attempts have been made to measure this efficiency and thereby the capacity of futures trading to provide information on future spot prices.

On the empirical side, various studies have attempted to measure the accuracy with which prices have been forecast in markets with futures trading. The general conclusion, which should be intuitively clear, is that the longer the forecast period (i.e., involving futures of more distant months), the more subject to error will be the predictions of futures prices. Also, some recent investigations have concluded that the existence of active futures markets promotes more efficient operation of the spot market such that spot prices tend to converge to more "informationally efficient" equilibria.

On the conceptual side, there are three basic questions about the information-spreading role of the futures markets. First, does the market actually convey all the information from those who have it to those who do not have it? Second, do the "owners" of information have enough incentive to transfer their knowledge to other people? If the information these owners possess becomes public through the transactions they pursue in the futures markets, they soon lose their comparative advantage (of having more accurate information), with no assurance that they have been compensated for their efforts in acquiring the information. Third, can the information not be transferred through the spot market, and should there be anything left for the futures prices to reflect?

The first and the second questions stated above do not lead to enough reasons to invalidate the information role of futures prices, because one can advance the counter-argument that speculators release only part of their information, for which they receive a return; thus, they will still have the incentive to continue their efforts in collecting information. However, the third reason remains valid. The existence of futures markets introduces the dimension of time into the price and extends the price-making horizon. But, at least in circumstances involving continuous inventories, forecasts are reflected just as much in cash and nearby futures as in distant futures prices.

THE THEORY OF NORMAL BACKWARDATION

A classical hypothesis in futures market analysis is that futures prices are estimates of the spot price at maturity biased in a downward direction. Viewing speculators as insurers who receive a risk premium from the hedgers, Keynes argued that "since in normal conditions the hedgers are not short, the expected spot price must exceed the futures price by the amount the hedger is willing to sacrifice to avoid the risk of price fluctuations." This argument has become known as the theory of normal backwardation.

The term *backwardation* is equivalent to what was called in previous sections "inverted market discount." In commodity trading, the British refer to any excess of the spot price over the futures price as backwardation, and this is, basically, where the term originates.

The question of the existence of a risk premium in the futures market has been extensively debated in the commodity-trading literature. On the theoretical side, the search for a risk premium has a close analogy in the insurance principle. The owner of an inventory, if he should wish to avoid any risk of a change in its value, might sell a futures contract against which that inventory is deliverable. He could expect to pay for the protection from the price risk so obtained, much as one must expect to pay for fire insurance. The major assumption of this theory is that the hedger is a risk-averse individual. Recent theoretical work has shown, however, that risk aversion is neither necessary nor sufficient for the existence of backwardation. As such, the theory of normal backwardation has lost the strong theoretical basis it once seemed to have.

On the empirical side, there have been numerous studies aimed at testing the theory of normal backwardation. Several of these studies have discovered evidence of trends in futures prices that can be associated with hedging patterns; the studies have further tried to attribute these trends to the existence of a risk premium. The factors involved in generating these patterns are, however, so numerous that one cannot separate the impact of risk on these patterns. Furthermore, some cross-market studies have concluded that price trends vary from one market to another without any relation to the level of risk. This, of course, does not mean that there is no bias in futures prices acting as an estimator of the spot price on the maturity date. Conversely, most empirical studies have found that such a bias does exist. Its relationship with risk is not clear, however, and, thus, it cannot be viewed as a risk premium.

Although it is generally accepted that futures markets are used by risk-averse hedgers, the risk premium, if any, is insignificant. This means hedgers purchase the insurance very cheaply. Thus, one would not expect speculators to make considerable profits. Speculators do, however, make money, and this is the reason they keep on participating in futures trading. The question then is, What are the factors that determine the speculator's return on futures market activity?

Research has shown that speculators do not make money according to the method suggested by the normal backwardation theory. In the majority of cases examined, it has been found that only large speculators make substantial and consistent profits. Small speculators are often losers. They lose to large speculators or hedgers. This finding has led some analysts to view the speculators' profits as returns to forecasting ability. According to this view, speculation is a skilled occupation and not just a risk-bearing act. The return on speculation varies greatly with the ability and knowledge of the speculator. Since large speculators are more likely to be endowed with forecasting expertise, they are expected to gain more profit than the small speculators.

THE IMPACT OF FUTURES TRADING ON THE STABILITY OF THE SPOT MARKET PRICE

The impact of speculation on price stability has long been subject to academic as well as public discussion. Traditionally, speculation was viewed as creating unjustified price levels and undesirable price fluctuations. According to this belief, professional speculators "go with the market." When a price movement has begun for whatever reason, professionals follow the movement and thereby reinforce it. They abuse the mass psychology of the public to make a profit and at the same time amplify this mass psychology.

The contemporary belief, however, is that futures trading encourages specialization in the activities of assembling and interpreting market information. Thus, it can be expected to improve the performance of the spot market. This belief is especially reinforced by several scholarly works that have, theoretically and/or empirically, shown that futures trading improves the allocation of resources over time even if producers do not participate in the futures market but only use the price information provided by futures trading.

Both theoretical and empirical studies on the impact of futures trading on the stabilization of the cash market price are based on two distinct issues:

• The role that futures trading plays in risk sharing; and
• The information that futures trading provides to producers, processors, and stockpilers.

The results of empirical research on the impact of the risk-sharing role of futures trading on the stability of the spot market price have been controversial. They have had a slight tendency to support a stabilizing role for futures markets "that have reached a mature stage."

On the other hand, the results of research on the impact of the informational role of futures trading on the stability of the cash market price have been conclusive. They indicate that futures trading transmits the informed traders' information to all economic agents, especially producers and processors. This transfer provides a link between the variations in supply and demand, thereby stabilizing spot market prices.

Exhibit 10.2
The Impact of Futures Market Operations on the Stability of Spot Prices

---

Through the risk-sharing role

- The effect is not clear.
- Empirical research has a slight tendency towards supporting a stabilizing effect.

Through the information provision role

- The futures market stabilizes the spot price.
- Its stabilizing effect is more important in markets with a scattered and decentralized structure.
- The stabilizing effect materializes where the futures market has reached a mature stage.

CHAPTER **11**

Predicting Futures Prices: Science versus Art

FUNDAMENTAL ANALYSIS IN QUESTION

Economists are sometimes surprised to see that commodity traders ignore supply and demand factors and rely on a very simplistic time-trend analysis to predict the future pattern of prices. They are even more surprised when they see that these simplistic methods often work.

From the viewpoint of traders in the futures market, price forecasting techniques can be grouped into two broad categories: fundamental analysis and chart analysis. The latter category is also referred to as "technical analysis." Fundamental analysis is based on the economic concepts of supply and demand. It normally takes account of possible changes in production, consumption, and the import and export of a commodity. Included in this analysis is the impact of political events on supply and demand. In utilizing this approach, the analyst postulates a set of equations and attempts to assess (objectively or subjectively) the impact of variations in the factors affecting the worldwide and domestic markets of a commodity. Thus, international, political, and economic factors are used to predict the price of the commodity.

Chart or technical analysis has a much narrower scope than fundamental analysis: it takes account of very few characteristics of the market. Most technical analysts reject the use of supply and demand behavior to predict price. They believe that price swings indicate whether prices are going higher or lower: the basic idea is that "the way the market behaved yesterday indicates how it may behave today." Thus, technical analysts use the data generated by the futures market to forecast future prices by charting the price trend. They are not concerned with data on other supply- and demand-related variables. Many chartists believe that by beginning to consider the variations in the supply and demand factors they would begin "to lose the game the moment they take their eyes off the chart." In their view, supply and demand statistics, as well as news events, are all subject to personal evaluation. Thus, each person interprets the information differently and arrives at a different conclusion with regard to the short-term price changes. Further, most of this information is known to traders before it becomes public. Thus, its impact may already be incorporated in the current price. In other words, chartists view the current price trend as a comprehensive indicator of all the fundamental information that statistical analysts can hope to learn.

In addition, the price trend is believed to contain two other aspects of the market not incorporated in fundamental analysis. First, there is significant inside information in any trade which is secret to the public but is known to some traders. These traders use the information to arrive at their trade decisions. The resultant price will then reflect part of this information. Second, the psychology of the market, which is often difficult to incorporate in fundamental analysis, is to a large extent reflected by the price pattern. The psychology of the trading public often works in an unexpected manner. A news event that logically should have only a marginal impact on the market may suddenly result in an enormous change in market conditions through the accumulative reactions of the public. Conversely, the trading public may choose not to react to the release of information that will have a significant impact on the market.

Faced with such complications in price forecasting, chartists suggest that an "understanding of the price pattern is equivalent to understanding all aspects of the market." This statement is, in general, true. If the price pattern is understood, so is the behavior of the market. As is explained in the following sections of this chapter, a chartist's way of following and understanding the price pattern is, however, a "special way" and does not carry the general implications of price analysis. This special way is limited merely to keeping a record of past prices, and watching, in a mechanical sense, the way the price has increased or decreased. It provides an insight into the very short-term variations of the price but has no capability to forecast long-term or even medium-term price patterns. However, the main concern of traders is short-term price changes. They adhere to the so-called technical analysis to arrive at their trading decisions.

The politico-economic dimensions of the petroleum market provide a unique status for futures trading in the petroleum market compared with other commodities. Prediction of petroleum futures prices cannot be based solely on price charts. Instead, one should choose a composite view of price charts and fundamental analysis to assess the pattern of petroleum futures prices. While petroleum market analysts are accustomed to using fundamental analysis, they are not very familiar with the price-charting techniques. The remainder of this chapter provides a description of these techniques as well as examples of their application to petroleum futures.

THE DAILY BAR CHARTS

Many methods exist for displaying price movements. The daily bar chart is the simplest and the most common of these techniques. It shows clearly price movements from one day to the next. The updating of this chart is also very simple and inexpensive. Only a few minutes a day are needed to maintain and update a chart of petroleum futures prices.

Price bar charts show the daily high, daily low, and the closing price of futures contracts. An example of this type of chart is shown in Figure 11.1. It shows the price of crude oil contracts in a typical period. Along the horizontal axis, the lines are marked with each trading date, while weekends and holidays are omitted to keep the continuity of the price trend. For each day, a vertical line is drawn between the highest and the lowest price of that day. A short horizontal bar is then added to show the closing price.

Price bar charts can be drawn based on daily variations (as shown in Figure 11.1), weekly changes, or even monthly trends. A weekly bar chart shows the highest, lowest, and the closing price during each week. The monthly bar chart depicts the same information for each month. It is normally desirable to keep a weekly as well as a daily bar chart to provide a better perspective of the price pattern.

Finally, it should be pointed out that the closing price may often involve a split. This means that in the last few seconds of trading, a particular contract was traded by various brokers at somewhat different prices. In such a case, the closing price will not be unique and the bar

Figure 11.1
Daily Bar Chart of a Crude Oil Contract Traded on NYMEX in a
Typical Period

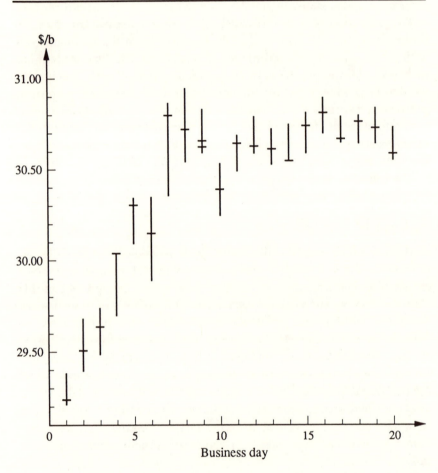

is crossed with two horizontal lines (instead of one). These lines will
show the upper and the lower levels of the closing price.

POINT-AND-FIGURE CHARTS

Some chartists maintain that the information provided by a bar chart
(i.e., the highest, lowest, and closing prices) is not sufficient to arrive at
a relatively accurate prediction of the future price. Instead, they look
for the prices at which most of the buying and selling took place during

each day. They believe these prices carry much more important information than the highest and lowest prices included in a bar chart.

A "point-and-figure" chart records all price movements of each trading day. Clearly, maintaining point-and-figure charts would require much more time than the time needed to update a single bar chart. To maintain a point-and-figure chart, one has to watch the trading record all day long. Further, the information required for this type of chart has to be acquired through a special service agreement, while the figures needed for a single bar chart are readily available in the daily business papers.

Preparation of the point-and-figure charts is time-consuming, but straightforward. The vertical axis of the point-and-figure chart shows the price in the same way as the bar chart.

The following example, using the various prices quoted for crude oil during a trading day, will show how point-and-figure charts are constructed. The opening price of crude oil was $30.30/b. It then traded downward to $29.90/b and up to $30.30/b. Finally, it moved down to close at $30.10/b. Figure 11.2 shows the same information on a point-and-figure chart. Each box in this figure represents $0.10. The chart begins with $30.30/b and goes down to $29.90/b. After the market has traded down to $29.90/b, it rallies and trades back to $30.00/b. One should, therefore, fill in the $30.00 box. However, this has already been filled in on the way down. Thus, a new column has to be used. This is the $30.00 space in the next column. The same procedure is then continued. The other boxes of the second column are filled in according to the prices quoted on the market until it is necessary to move to the third column. This happens when the price falls from $30.30 to $30.20/b. The subsequent price is $30.10/b, which is also the closing price. It is customary to mark the closing price by shading the corresponding box. The next day's trade opens at $30.20/b, rallies to $30.90/b, and closes at $30.80/b.

Obviously, each column of a point-and-figure chart does not necessarily show the prices quoted on the same trading day. Several columns may represent the prices of a single trading day. Also, one column may contain the prices quoted on several days. A new column is not begun simply because of a new day's price. Each column is used until a space that has already been marked must be filled in. Then the next column is used. As Figure 11.2 shows, a closing price of $30.80/b is included in column E. The opening price on the next day is $30.90/b, which is again included in column E.

Figure 11.2
Point-and-Figure Chart for the Crude Oil Price

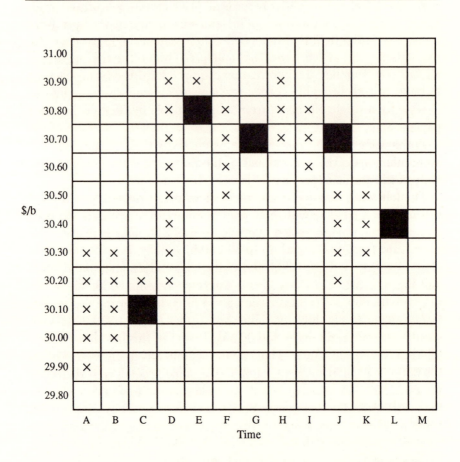

The point-and-figure chart shows the frequency of each price as quoted in the market in the recent past. It presents the price information in much greater detail than does the daily bar chart. The point-and-figure chart is not, however, a substitute for the daily bar chart. It is an expensive tool that some technical analysts use when the price is very volatile and its hour-by-hour pattern should be traced to provide a feel for future price changes.

Although the point-and-figure chart contains a considerable amount of information about the price, it may confuse the trader because it contains too many small variations in the price. Some of these variations may be nothing more than random fluctuations. The trader who is looking for a buy or sell signal may then act upon these variations and consequently lose because of the false move. To avoid such confusion, many chartists try to eliminate the minor fluctuations by choosing a price scale that is greater than the minimum fluctuation permitted for the price of the commodity. As stated in chapter 7, the minimum price fluctuation for crude oil is $0.01/b. The scale that was chosen for Figure 11.2 is $0.10/b—that is, many price quotations indicating a small price change have been eliminated. In this way, the point-and-figure chart becomes less crowded and less confusing. This scale is chosen to cope with the wide range of variations in the crude oil price during the corresponding period. Clearly, the scale should be adjusted to fit the situation of the period under study.

Another method for eliminating minor fluctuations of the price trend is to record a price reversal, but only if the trend is reversed by more than a predetermined magnitude. For example, if a chartist decides not to record a price change before the amount of reversal exceeds $0.20/b, he will not record any of these price quotations—$30.70, $30.80, $30.85, $30.75, $30.70, and $30.80—as valid changes in price. To the same chartist, all these price quotations—$30.70, $30.80, $30.90, $30.80, and $30.70—are considered valid price changes and will be included in the point-and-figure chart. As with the "scale-change" method, the predetermined magnitude depends on the extent of price fluctuations in the period under study. Under normal conditions (when the price volatility is low), the predetermined amount for price reversal may be from $0.03 to $0.05/b. A rather standard way of imposing a reversal condition is to choose a predetermined amount equal to three times the minimum price fluctuation while keeping the chart scale at this minimum level.

In short, the point-and-figure chart is actually much more flexible than it initially sounds. One can easily adjust the details of price information contained in this type of chart to specific needs by choosing a proper scale and a predetermined reversal condition.

THE MOVING-AVERAGE METHOD

Some technical analysts view the daily variations of the price as minor fluctuations around a major price trend; they purport to discover the major trend. They view the minor fluctuations in a bar chart, and especially those contained in a point-and-figure-chart, as "noise" that may cause the major trend to be missed. Thus, these technical analysts suggest a moving-average method that is presumably based on a broader perspective of price patterns than the bar chart or the point-and-figure chart shows.

The moving-average method disregards the "within-day" fluctuations and smooths the daily ups and downs in the price trend. The advantage of this method is the possible elimination of confusing variations in the price. In eliminating some price information, however, one would risk losing useful as well as useless information. The average trend that is derived will entail a time lag with regard to the turning points in the price pattern. Thus, on many occasions, the analyst will declare a price reversal when it is probably too late to take advantage of the change in the trend. The advocates of the moving-average method, however, argue that this problem does not jeopardize the usefulness of the moving-average method. The main value of this method is not in picking up the top or bottom of the move but in trying to determine the longer-term trends. The method is designed to limit losses when the trader is on the wrong side of the market and to accumulate profits by staying with the market when the trader has a good forecast of the trend.

To construct the moving-average trend, technical analysts use a time series of closing prices. The period of averaging may vary from a few days to a few weeks. Many traders keep several trends, each of which relays some information about the price movement.

Figure 11.3 shows the closing price of heating oil in a typical period. The closing price on the first business day is \$0.8155 per gallon. On the next business day, the closing price increases to \$0.8250, and on the third day it reaches \$0.8337 per gallon. The average of these three prices will be \$0.8247—(\$0.8155 + \$0.8250 + \$0.8337)/3 = \$0.8247 per gallon—which is one point on the (three-day) moving-average curve. The fourth day's closing price is \$0.8340 per gallon. The (three-day) moving-average is now calculated as the average of \$0.8250, \$0.8337, and \$0.8340, which is \$0.8309. This value is shown as the second point on the (three-day) moving-average curve. The method of calculating the moving average should be clear by now. The average of the closing prices of the most recent three days is calculated. As a new price is considered, the earliest price is eliminated. This is the reason the method is called a moving average.

Figure 11.3 shows several important features of the moving-average method. First, whenever the market advances by a certain amount, the average value advances by a smaller margin. Second, if the market de-

Figure 11.3
Daily Price, and Three-Day, Five-Day, and Ten-Day Moving-Average Prices of a Heating Oil Contract Traded on NYMEX in a Typical Period

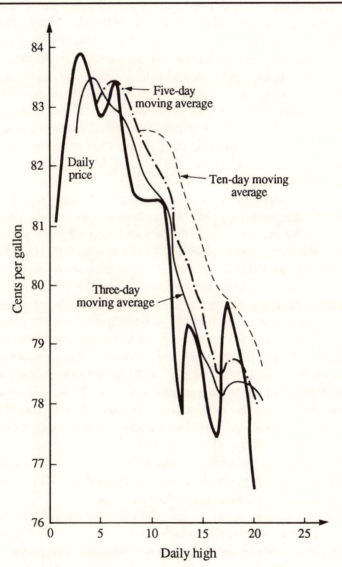

clines by a specific value, the average figure decreases by a smaller magnitude. Third, when the market reverses downward, the average trend may continue to advance. If the price decline sustains, then the average will turn down. This characteristic is also observed if the market reverses upward. That is, on both the upside and downside, the average price lags behind the daily market price.

The moving-average trend helps the trader determine the timing of liquidating the long position and establishing a short position. The trader will clearly hold his long position as long as the moving average continues to advance. When the average reverses downward, the trader liquidates his long position and establishes a short position. As mentioned earlier, there is a lag between the turning phase of the average curve relative to the reversal of the daily price. This lag is not very long in the case of a three-day moving average. As can be seen in Figure 11.3, it is, however, quite significant for a ten-day or even five-day moving average. One way to cope with this lag is to use the moving-average trend along with the daily price pattern.

Several approaches can be used to combine the daily price pattern with the moving-average trend. The easiest one is to plot the daily closing price on same chart as the moving-average trend. Figure 11.3 shows the daily closing price and the three-day moving average trend. The daily price starts to decline on day four while the moving average is still advancing. A simple rule of thumb used by traders is to liquidate the long positions when the two curves cross on day five. In other words, long positions are not liquidated just because the daily closing price shows a reversal on day four. Neither is the liquidation postponed until the average turns downward. Instead, the trader chooses a point between the two. That is, on day five he has enough indication of a price downturn to liquidate his long position. Nevertheless, he is not so confident in the price downtrend as to establish a short position in the market. The short position is established after the moving-average trend begins to decline on day six.

The second approach to combining the moving average and the daily price chart is to show the daily price range (and not just the daily closing price) on the same chart as the moving-average trend. This will provide the trader with a tool to analyze the price variation each day. He can then compare the variation with the longer-term price movement to make appropriate decisions during a trading day. The problem with this approach is that the within-day price fluctuation may cross the average trend several times, leading to inconsistent sell-and-buy signals that

Figure 11.4
Three-Day Moving Averages of Daily Low and Daily High Prices of a
Heating Oil Contract Traded on NYMEX in a Typical Period

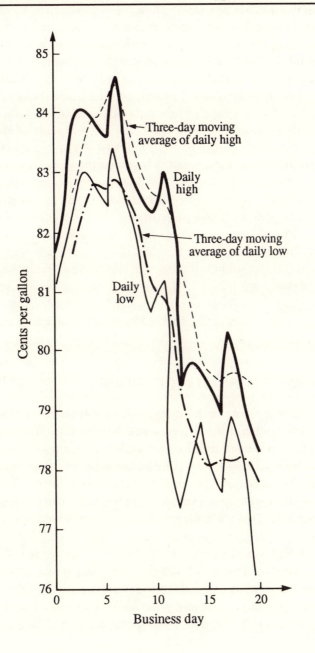

confuse the trader. To avoid such confusion, the trader should choose an arbitrary amount below and/or above which the daily range must go before he decides to take a trading action.

The third approach is to base the moving-average calculations on the daily high and daily low (and not on the closing price). In this way, the trader will have two moving-average curves: one corresponding to the daily low and the other associated with the daily high (see Figure 11.4). Between these two curves is a rather wide band within which the daily prices tend to vary. If the price moves outside of this band, it is likely that a new price pattern is formed, on which the trader will base his buying or selling action. As in the previous approach, the trader chooses an arbitrary amount. Should the price move outside of the amount's band, this would indicate the development of a new price pattern. The choice of this arbitrary amount is based on the trader's subjective evaluation of what constitutes a normal price fluctuation. His evaluation will be based on the extent of price fluctuations in the recent past.

In addition to the above three approaches, many other methods can be used to combine the various forms of moving-average trends with each other or with daily prices. Most of them are, however, simple variations of the approaches discussed in this section. What is important is to understand the basics of the moving-average trend. Beyond that, each trader may develop his own approach in using the moving-average trend in conjunction with other information to arrive at trading decisions.

SUPPORT AND RESISTANCE AREAS

When the price of a certain commodity continues to decline for a considerable period of time, it begins to show resistance to any further decline. The reason is straightforward and can be shown by example. Most refiners hesitate to buy new crude oil during a period of declining prices because they assume they can obtain the crude cheaper the next week or the next month. However, to cope with production requirements when the level of stock has been drawn to a minimum, the purchase of crude can no longer be postponed. Some refiners will then begin to buy crude oil. The developing demand of these refineries may halt the progressive price decline. Other refiners, who may not have been forced to buy the crude, would be induced to purchase some of their crude requirements because they have some indication as to when the price decline will cease. The process may go on for a considerable period of time. Buyers and sellers are both uncertain about the future price, but both try to avoid a price risk through limited participation in market activities. The market will establish a temporary equilibrium around a certain price level, and daily prices will fluctuate within a limited range around this price level. Traders refer to such a situation as a "congestion area."

The existence of a congestion area is not limited to the case of a downward price movement. In general, a congestion area may develop when the price has reached a minimum or a maximum level. In addition, a congestion area may occasionally interrupt either a downward or an upward price movement. That is, congestion areas may be encountered anywhere on the price chart. They merely indicate that the price is somehow temporarily stuck around a specific value. However, when this congestion appears around a maximum price level, the area is referred to as a "resistance area." Conversely, when the congestion appears around a minimum price, the area is known as a "support area." It follows that when a trend turns downward, a congestion area that functioned as "resistance" during the initial uptrend will now become a support area.

The idea of resistance and support prices can further be expanded to arrive at more comprehensive price patterns. Analyses of these price patterns are based on the uptrend and downtrend lines. The uptrend line shows the lower limits of price fluctuations during a period of rising prices. The downtrend line shows the upper limits of the price fluctuations during a period of falling prices.

To construct a downward line, the chartist draws a line connecting the high points (A and B in Figure 11.5). This line indicates an upper limit to price variations. So long as the downward movement continues, the line is not penetrated. When a price such as point C is observed, the chartist receives an initial indication that the price trend may change. He waits, however, for a confirming signal before he acts on this change. As Figure 11.5 shows, the downtrend continues and point C is ignored. The next indication for a change in the trend is observed when the price closes at level D. Again, the trader waits for a confirming signal. After passing through a congestion area, he receives enough confirming signals to indicate that the price is heading upward. By connecting the lowest points (F and G) of this new trend, the chartist arrives at the uptrend line, which will establish a lower limit to price fluctuations.

As with other charting techniques, the trend-line method does not lead the trader to foresee the top or the bottom of a price trend. There-

Figure 11.5
The Dowtrend and Uptrend Lines

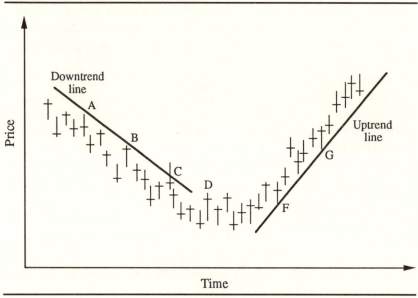

fore, the chart trader will never sell at the maximum price nor buy at the minimum price. Only after a trend appears to be under way does the trader enter the market to take advantage of this trend. He will sell his long position only after the chart indicates the upward trend has ended. In the same manner, he will buy (back) his short position after the chart shows the downtrend has ended.

CONCLUSION

Disregarding all the available information about market forces and relying solely on price chart formations is, of course, too extreme to accept. There are, however, enough reasons to believe that, under special circumstances, chart analysis may provide useful guidelines for futures trading. First, if a significant number of traders use this type of analysis, then just the fact that these methods signal a buy or sell decision may have an impact on the price. After a signal is given, the traders would follow the directives generated by the technical analysis and, in so doing, may cause some change in the price. That is, though the procedure itself has no scientific value, it may push the price in the direction it has predicted. Second, when price behavior undergoes some structural shifts, price prediction may be performed more efficiently if it is based on observation of the recent past as opposed to the long-term time series normally used in the econometric modeling of supply and demand.

To summarize, the chartist's approach to price prediction is not totally nonscientific. Furthermore, this approach is often used as a practical tool to arrive at futures trading decisions. It should not, however, be viewed as the only alternative. Rather, it can be utilized in conjunction with fundamental analysis. The analyst should first determine, through an appraisal of supply and demand conditions, the probable course of prices. If he arrives, for example, at the conclusion that the price is too low, then he can examine the chart to determine when he should buy futures contracts and when he should limit his losses in the event his appraisal of market conditions is wrong.

CHAPTER 12

OPEC, Spot, and Futures Trading: A New Market Triangle

IS OPEC MANIPULATING THE SPOT PRICE OR IS THE SPOT PRICE MANIPULATING OPEC?

Today there is hardly anything more important in OPEC's functioning as the market coordinator than the spot market price of crude oil. Perhaps this has always been the case, but the nature of the interaction between OPEC and the spot market has changed over time, as has the status of OPEC in the international petroleum market. This interaction has passed through five distinct episodes, each marked by different policy aims:

- *Price following (1973–81)*. OPEC assumes the role of price administrator but does little to administer the price; spot prices are set by the course of events; OPEC follows price changes with a lag.
- *Price control (1982–March 1983)*. OPEC decides to control the price by adjusting the supply; downward spot price trends are reversed several times by OPEC's announcement of a production prorationing scheme.
- *Revenue control (March 1983–third quarter 1985)*. OPEC realizes that absolute control of a fixed price is not feasible; it decides to adjust prices and production simultaneously to support revenues.
- *Market share (fourth quarter 1985–December 1986)*. Price control is abandoned in favor of market share, marked by a move towards netback trading.

- *Price control (December 1986–present)*. OPEC returns to a policy of fixed price with rather strict monitoring of the supply.

Price Following (1973–81)

During this episode OPEC had substantial potentials to control the market but did not utilize these potentials. Its "price administration" policies were merely coincidental and were based on the ad hoc subjective actions of its individual members. There was no formal sharing of an agreed production quota. The only instance in which cutbacks were decided collectively, not by OPEC but by some of its Arab members, was the embargo of 1973–74, which was a political act limited in its scope and objectives. The embargo was not undertaken for price reasons.

At any point in time the market price and the level of supply are two sides of the same equation. If the level of supply (or demand) is free of control, so has to be the price. It was not surprising then that during the period 1973–81 OPEC defended a price as long as it did not have to expend much effort in doing so; when it did, OPEC simply abandoned the price and followed the market. The mechanics of price administration were as follows. The spot price was set by a host of factors, including political events, expectations of future price patterns, change in real demand, inventory buildup, etc. Small variations in the spot price went unnoticed and were absorbed by the oil companies, which acted as intermediaries between OPEC producers and the petroleum market. Significant variations, however, prompted two distinct reactions in the market:

- Buyers would ask producers for higher or lower levels of offtake depending on whether the spot prices were above or below the official price; and
- Non-OPEC producers, notably North Sea since the late 1970s, responded to the market price by adjusting their official prices.

The above two reactions made some OPEC producers, particularly African producers who competed directly with North Sea producers, adjust their prices. The adjustment by individual members was normally in the form of discounts and premiums over the reference (Arab Light) price. Finally, after most members had already adjusted their prices to reflect the variations in spot prices, an OPEC conference was held to recognize publicly what had been happening all along.

The period included a mild slackening (mid-1977 to mid-1978), the Iranian crisis (from late 1978 to 1980), and a period of rapid decline in demand (1981). The slack period bypassed OPEC without significantly affecting its production and pricing policy. The Iranian crisis and the period of decline tested OPEC's price control capability in both upward and downward market trends. In June 1979 OPEC raised its posted price to $18.00/b after the spot market had hit $34.00/b. It also allowed member countries to add to the prices of their crude a maximum premium of $2.00 over and above their normal differentials, if and when necessitated by market conditions. The OPEC communiqué also stated that the price charged by any member should not exceed $23.50/b. The official price was then raised to $24.00 in November 1979 and by increments of $2.00 every quarter, reaching $32.00/b in February 1981. All of the price increases followed the spot market price. From February to the end of 1981, OPEC's official price was adjusted once in October 1981 to $34.00/b, while the spot price declined from about $40.00 to $32.00/b in midyear before recovering to $34.00/b in the last quarter of 1981. The perception at the time was that the market had reached its equilibrium at $34.00/b. Although the question of crude price differentials was still undecided, OPEC was thought to have succeeded in bringing order to the market. OPEC had held numerous meetings but had taken little real action, such as restricting production, to achieve this success. In fact, OPEC members followed conflicting production policies: in 1980–81, when the market began to soften (the "mini-glut" as it was called at the time), Libya, Kuwait, and Algeria reduced their outputs while Saudi Arabia continued to produce at close to its maximum capacity of 10 million b/d.

Price Control (1982–March 1983)

In the first quarter of 1982, due to overstocking in the previous year and sluggish demand, the spot price fell from $34.00 to $28.00/b. All oil companies and producing countries hoped that Saudi Arabia would act to defend OPEC's $34.00/b benchmark. In the meantime, price cutting began. North Sea crude was discounted by $2.50–3.00/b in early February, and Iran, Egypt, Mexico, and Venezuela discounted their crudes by $1.00–2.50/b in late February and early March 1982. Contract prices for U.S. crude declined to an Arab Light equivalent of $30.00/b. By the time OPEC convened in the second half of March, the view in oil industry circles was that OPEC's $34.00/b target could not be held and that OPEC would have to cut its benchmark price to $28.00/b. Instead,

OPEC decided in its March meeting to "defend" $34.00/b by limiting production to 17.5 million b/d. This opened a new chapter in OPEC's history. It was the first time that OPEC had collectively agreed to set a total oil production level and to allocate it among its members. A Market Monitoring Committee was formed to review market development and recommend action on prices and supply immediately before each conference. This marked the birth of OPEC as a formal cartel. It immediately had some success. The spot price went back to $34.00/b for two months. This was followed by a relapse; but OPEC succeeded in engineering a second recovery to $34.00/b in September, strengthening the perception that it was capable of managing the spot price by choosing appropriate production policies. In late 1982 and early 1983, however, it became apparent that most OPEC members were not taking production quotas seriously; spot prices declined to $28.00–29.00/b.

Revenue Control (March 1983–Third Quarter 1985)

This episode marks a period of reappraisal. Production quotas had to be accepted and implemented by all members. In addition, downward adjustment of official prices was recognized as necessary to realign supply and demand. The price cut in March 1983 was OPEC's first significant retreat. It was, however, a strategic retreat, and part of a scheme whereby the new price was to be supported from further downward pressure by a schedule of production quotas within an overall output limit of 17.5 million b/d. The scheme, however fragile and artificially based, was a qualified success. The lower benchmark price together with the accepted production constraints (or at least the perception that they were being adhered to) led to the longest period of price stability since the price chaos of 1979–81. Spot prices in the period March 1983–May 1984 stayed around the official price; product prices were also steady. OPEC regained some credibility. Even non-OPEC members did not react to spot prices hastily; they waited for OPEC to take the corrective action and bring the spot price back in line with the official price.

In mid-1984, a price fall was reversed by joint OPEC/non-OPEC action, but in the fourth quarter a series of problems, beginning with difficulty in grading crude differentials and extending into a set of unbelievable misunderstandings between Saudi Arabia, North Sea producers, and Nigeria, set off further declines in the spot price and thereby increased the pressure on OPEC's marker crude price, then at

$29.00/b. After announcing several supply cutbacks, which were not fully observed by all members, OPEC launched a "last ditch" effort to reestablish its credibility in the oil marketplace and salvage its role as manager of the world oil price structure. In January 1985, a high-powered OPEC inner cabinet, the Ministerial Executive Council, was formed to monitor member states' compliance with agreed production and pricing policy. The council hired an independent firm of auditors, Klynveld Kraayenhof, to audit the members' books and practices and to provide the council with information on overproduction and marketing malpractices of the members. Later, the council was given authority to demand compliance on the part of members caught cheating by the auditor. With the new arrangement in place and announcement by OPEC of a production ceiling of 16 million b/d and a $1.00/b reduction in price, new hopes were raised that market prices would begin to behave. After a few months of instability, a stable trend seemed to emerge—but at the cost to OPEC of an oil output limited to 16 million b/d. For the Saudis, who had become exasperated by the cheating of other OPEC members, the fall to 2 million b/d in mid-1985 was the last straw. In the third quarter of 1985 Saudi Arabia withdrew from its role as swing producer. It also warned that it would follow the lead of other countries if they continued to cheat. The warning, which had been given several times before, was taken more seriously this time; at a July 1985 meeting, all members of OPEC agreed to end marketing malpractices. This agreement, along with surprisingly firm spot prices in August, allowed OPEC, and the market, to enter the fourth quarter rather smoothly. Even if Saudi Arabia had abandoned the role of swing producer, as the thinking went at the time, OPEC as a whole should have been able to play the role of swing producer without a radical reshuffling of output quotas.

Market Share (Fourth Quarter 1985–December 1986)

The fourth quarter of 1985 was the beginning of another new era for OPEC and the oil industry. Confusingly, it began with high prices but continued with Saudi Arabia abandoning price and revenue support in favor of market share, leading OPEC and the rest of the world into the third oil shock.

The spot prices of the two key non-OPEC crudes, Brent and WTI, continued to rise during October and November 1985, hitting the highest level since 1982 and yielding premiums of up to $2.00/b above official prices. Encouraged by this, OPEC member countries:

- Increased outputs substantially above quotas, and
- Sold an increasing proportion of their output at market-related prices with no apparent harm: spot prices remained close to or even above the official price.

By mid-November, OPEC output reached 18 million b/d, the highest level since July 1984. At least nine of OPEC's thirteen members were exceeding official quotas. Nigeria's output was about 1.7 million b/d, compared with 1.68 million b/d in October and 1.5 million b/d in September, and with a quota of 1.3 million b/d. The United Arab Emirate's output reached 1.25 million b/d of crude, plus some 50,000 b/d of condensates, exceeding its quota by around 300,000 b/d. Libya, at 1.2 million b/d, was 200,000 barrels over quota. Iraq, with Red Sea sales running at 400,000 b/d, boosted production to 1.7 million b/d, 500,000 b/d over the official ceiling; and Iran, in spite of Iraqi attacks on Kharg Island, was producing 2.3 million b/d and still trying to boost sales in December. Saudi Arabia, which had initially sought to increase its output from 2.3 to 3.5 million b/d, raised its production close to the quota of 4.3 million b/d.

The market was being flooded with oil, but the spot price, according to the usual indicators, held up until early December. The first signs of the increased production reached *Platt's* and other market monitors in the first week of December, just before OPEC's 76th Ordinary Conference in Geneva (December 7–9, 1985). Spot prices were not soft enough to create any alarm among producers at the meeting. What was of real concern was the longer-term prospect—in particular, the belief that output would have to be cut back by 3–4 million b/d in order to keep supply and demand in balance in 1986. This was the background against which the most important decision in OPEC's recent history was made: the conference decided unanimously to abandon OPEC's role as the world's swing producer. The decision was made with much less quarrel and in a much shorter time than might have been expected. This could imply that most OPEC members were assuming that the real edge of the knife was directed towards non-OPEC producers, but they had underestimated the potential damage to themselves. This could very well be the case for some members, particularly those who still felt the comfort of the prevailing firm spot prices, but at least Saudi Arabia seemed aware of and prepared to deal with the consequences of what was going to happen.

OPEC's announcement produced a mixed reaction on spot market prices. A sudden decline from $30.00 to $22.00/b was short-lived. Prices stabilized around $26.00/b in a matter of a few days, and the oil market community tended to regard OPEC's announcement as a bluff. Non-OPEC members responded to OPEC's call for output restraint with a deafening silence. Both the U.K. and Norwegian governments remained more concerned with sustaining development than with the revenue implications of tumbling prices; Mexico responded by announcing an effort to boost output by 200,000 to 300,000 b/d. Underpinning these reactions was the view that:

- OPEC, whatever it might say, had neither the strength nor the stamina to fight and win a price war for market share; and
- OPEC did not have a mechanism to turn the theory into practice—OPEC could not produce if refiners refused to buy.

The collapse of the spot market began in late January 1986 when it became clear that a price war had really broken out and that most OPEC members had changed to market-responsive pricing of their crude in order to take the risk off refiners, thereby encouraging them to lift the increased OPEC production.

Saudi Arabia's role as swing producer within OPEC, which was itself a residual supplier, had given Saudi Arabia the task of coping single-handedly with declining demand. A decline of 1 percent in the world's total energy consumption of about 200 million b/d of oil equivalent, while nonoil energy supplies continued to increase, led to a reduction in demand for oil of about 2 million b/d. With no reduction in supply from non-OPEC producers, the entire 2 million b/d had to be met by OPEC, and most of it by Saudi Arabia. This was the mechanism that squeezed Saudi output from 10 million b/d in 1981 to 2.3 million b/d in the third quarter of 1985, and which would have forced Saudi output down perhaps to 1.5 million b/d in 1986.

The Saudi announcement in July 1985 that it was no longer willing to act as OPEC's swing producer was, at the time, viewed as just one more empty threat. The conventional wisdom in the oil market community was that after a sharp price decline in the first quarter of 1986, OPEC would, as it had always done, call for an emergency meeting in which all members would give their "normal" explanation of their inability or failure to cut back production; finally, Saudi Arabia would agree to cut back its output to 2–2.5 million b/d while other members would contribute cuts of a few hundred thousand barrels here and there.

Saudi Arabia had to plan to avoid such a resolution by:

- Establishing, somehow, that its intention to produce close to its quota of 4.3 million b/d was serious; and

- Installing a mechanism to sell its crude even when the market was declining and refiners simply would not lift.

Netback contracts provided a suitable means of dealing with both issues. There is little doubt that Saudi netback contracts elevated the bargaining position of Saudi Arabia within OPEC. They have also provided Saudi Arabia with a competitive edge to corner the market as other producers scramble to keep pace with plunging speculative spot markets. The more crucial question is, however, who won the price war?

The presumed objective of the war was to force non-OPEC producers to cooperate with OPEC in managing the oil market. But in practice the war was as much concerned with advocating for an integral discipline within OPEC. The environment for creating such discipline became prevalent rather quickly as OPEC members started to feel the financial pinch of lower oil prices. The financial impact of the price war varied among OPEC producers. Most vulnerable were those, such as Ecuador and Gabon, that had been producing at or close to capacity and that could not offset revenue losses with higher output. Next in line were Nigeria, Algeria, Qatar, Libya, and Indonesia, whose revenue dropped substantially as oil prices dropped below $20.00/b. At $15.00/b, far more countries began to encounter difficulties: Iran, Iraq, the United Arab Emirates, and, to some extent, Kuwait. Only Saudi Arabia appeared to be able to live with lower prices, although at less than $10.00/b even Saudi Arabia would not be able to maintain its already low 1985 oil revenue.[14] Nigeria had already been on the critical list of heavily indebted countries. With the collapse of oil prices, Indonesia, Venezuela, and Algeria were considered to be moving to a similar category. By the third quarter of 1986, only Saudi Arabia, Kuwait, and the United Arab Emirates seemed to have the financial strength, based on their foreign-exchange reserves, to continue the war.

The vulnerability of non-OPEC producers to the price war was highest among the Third World exporters, notably Mexico and Egypt. These countries agreed, almost immediately after the price war began, to cooperate with OPEC. The price battle was then aimed at forcing the North Sea producers to reduce their output. Again, among North Sea producers, the United Kingdom was the main target because of its hard political stance against cooperation with OPEC and its major share (2.6 out of 3.5 million b/d) in North Sea output. Thus, the real battle was to force the U.K. government to reduce the country's oil output, and this was the most difficult target of all. This was difficult not only because of the United Kingdom's political objective to "maintain the freest oil province in the world," but also because of the structure of the U.K. North Sea oil industry. The United Kingdom's output decisions, day to day, were made by private oil companies, which would reduce their production only if the market forced them to do so. This left OPEC with the following options:

- To displace part of the U.K. share in the world oil market by aggressive marketing; and
- To force U.K. producers out of business by cutthroat pricing.

The first option did not seem feasible. There was a highly organized market in North Sea oil, ensuring the sale of every cargo produced. The multiplicity of buyers, sellers, and traders of Brent would always make it the market to be cleared before other crudes. The integrated structure of many North Sea producers and their proximity to refiners provided a further incentive to lifting.

The second option would be feasible, but at what cost? The conventional wisdom is that in a competitive or free-market environment, current production will continue as long as revenues exceed short-run operating costs. In 1985 in the United Kingdom, these costs ranged between $1.46 and $14.30/b, with more than 75 percent of total output costing below $5.00, and more than one-half less than $2.00. These figures indicate that the price of oil had to drop below $5.00 a barrel before the U.K. producers would lower productive capacity to a significant extent.

By the time the price war ended in December 1986, most non-OPEC oil producers announced their explicit or implicit support for OPEC's reassuming control over prices. Immediately after the December 1986 OPEC accord to reestablish a fixed price of $18.00/b, Norway announced a temporary 7.5 percent cutback in its production, while Mexico, Egypt, the Soviet Union, Oman, Malaysia, and China indicated varying curbs to aid OPEC. The magnitude of the cutback by non-OPEC producers seemed less important than the act itself. OPEC had for the previous several years become frustrated by the attitude of non-OPEC producers, who, it seemed to OPEC, increased their output as much and as fast as they could, reaping where OPEC sowed and blaming OPEC when prices wobbled. The price war seems to have changed this attitude. The threat of OPEC's embarking on a price war, which was previously considered theoretical, is now viewed as practical. As a result, non-OPEC producers feel some responsibility in cooperating with OPEC's efforts to restrain output. Furthermore, the price war introduced a new element of uncertainty in projecting future prices, which discourages new exploration and development of alternative energy sources.

Probably, the most important outcome of the price war was the new discipline within OPEC. For more than two years, Saudi Arabia had become frustrated by the "irresponsible" marketing policies of some fellow members. The attitude of other members towards Saudi Arabia was similar to that of non-OPEC producers towards OPEC. The Saudis, they seemed to think, owed it to them to balance demand and supply. Saudi Arabia's freedom to adjust its output had become a burden rather than a privilege. The price war changed this attitude and has given Saudi Arabia the leverage to deal with other members of the organization. Saudi Arabia's ability to adjust production to cope with short-term swings in the market is still informally utilized, but its intention of keeping production close to its quota seems to be well understood and well respected.

FUTURES MARKETS AND OPEC

"Watch out OPEC. Here comes NYMEX, CBT, and IPE."
The Wall Street Journal, February 22, 1983

Petroleum futures had been in the market for several years when the New York Mercantile Exchange (NYMEX) and the Chicago Board of Trade (CBT) announced their intention to introduce crude oil contracts in February 1983. The argument advanced by trade analysts was that "the true value of crude oil will be increasingly determined by the nature of the futures markets' inherent system of open outcry rather than behind OPEC's closed doors." The mechanism envisaged for this shift of power in setting prices was:

- Futures prices should be set through open outcry of bids and offers in a competitive environment (the pit of an exchange);
- Futures prices should lead the spot price; and
- The spot price should determine OPEC's official price.

The first principle is not open to doubt. It describes the fundamentals of the workings of futures markets. The validity of the second and third principles is more difficult to ascertain. They normally apply in the short run but are not valid, at least in the above simplistic form, in the long run.

The relationship between spot and futures prices of various commodities has been studied by many analysts. The voluminous literature dealing with this subject is still far from conclusive. What is normally observed is a high correlation between spot and futures prices, but causality, and especially causality from futures to spot pricing, is absent. Theoretically, it has been shown that futures prices and spot prices are determined in a simultaneous manner, with cause and effect running both ways when the two markets are of comparable size. NYMEX crude oil trading has now reached an average level of 100 million b/d, which is considerably larger than the present spot market. Furthermore, petroleum futures prices have filled important shortcomings in the spot market's value as a source of information about oil prices. This is probably the main reason why petroleum futures prices have spread so fast and so far.

The third assumption, about the significance of the spot price in determining OPEC's official price, is more crucial than the assumption about spot and futures prices. Official OPEC prices have, in the medium term, been closely correlated with spot prices. This implies that the spot price and the official price influence one another. The nature of this influence has been very different in various periods. At times, OPEC has simply followed the spot price; at others, spot prices have clearly been influenced by OPEC decisions. In general, spot prices do not determine but, rather, they indicate the equilibrium price in the market. Supply and demand, on the other hand, determine the equilibrium price, and spot market transactions constitute the source of the industry's information about this price. OPEC uses this information to exercise its market power, and the market power itself depends on OPEC's ability to control its output. That is, for any level of OPEC output there is a market clearing price that would eventually prevail, with or without the spot market. The spot market declares this equilibrium price publicly. In this sense, petroleum futures markets serve the same function more effectively: they declare the equilibrium price rapidly and loudly. The rapid transmission of information through the futures market is sometimes accompanied by overreaction. But these are all of very short-term nature. Thus, the view that futures markets have taken the price determination power away from OPEC is unwarranted.

OPEC PARTICIPATION IN FUTURES TRADING

Having declared futures markets not guilty of OPEC coordination problems, one other aspect of futures market operations in relation to OPEC needs to be examined. Can OPEC use oil futures to strengthen its position in the petroleum market? What can OPEC expect to gain from participating in the futures market?

Possible incentives for OPEC to participate in the futures market are: (a) to make a speculative profit, (b) to hedge against a decline in the price of crude oil or refined products, and (c) to stabilize the spot market price.

Speculation

Like anyone else, OPEC could use the futures market for speculative gain. It might even be able to make large gains by engineering unexpected shifts in the spot price. OPEC would, however, find it difficult to do this often. It would either be unable to find parties prepared to enter contracts with it, or it would conceivably destroy the market altogether, by scaring off traders.

Hedging

The futures market is likely to offer OPEC equally few opportunities to insure against price falls by hedging. Gains or losses on futures contracts would be offset by the losses or gains in physical trade if OPEC's price was consistently adjusted to follow the spot market price. Since futures trading is short term in nature and the OPEC price normally deviates from the spot price in the short run, the hedge is not likely to be effective.

Spot Price Stabilization

A classic sequence of events in commodities markets begins with prices reacting to a short-term supply/demand imbalance. This prompts a sale or a scramble to buy petroleum stocks, accelerating the price movement. Intervention by OPEC on the futures market, by transferring the trade risks associated with one initial price movement from petroleum stockholders to itself, could reduce the incentive to sell or buy inventories and limit price volatility.

This could apply to crude or product markets equally. Most short-term fluctuations in the crude spot price are prompted by variations in product prices that are, in turn, related to sudden changes in the level of inventories, refinery utilization rates, etc. By participating in futures trading of oil products, OPEC could limit short-term fluctuations.

While OPEC can influence the spot market by buying and selling futures contracts, this influence can only be a moderating one. The futures market cannot provide OPEC with the means of keeping the spot price above its (supply-demand) equilibrium price. The futures market only enables OPEC to relieve the short-term fears that tend to reinforce price shifts. Longer-term trends are caused by the relationship between supply and demand. Futures trading cannot change these phenomena.

There are, however, several institutional barriers to OPEC's participation in futures trading:

- There is a limit to the number of contracts that OPEC can hold in U.S. exchanges.
- OPEC is required to establish one agency or agent to handle its futures trading.
- Successful trading in futures markets requires a rapid decision-making process.

Limits to the number of contracts that an entity can hold vary with the exchange in which one chooses to trade. In the United States, for example, the Commodity Futures Trading Commission (CFTC) requires each exchange to impose a limit on the number of contracts (net short or net long) that any person or "persons acting in concert" can hold. This limit is to prevent traders, such as OPEC, from manipulating market prices.

At present, NYMEX limits the number of contracts that any agent can hold to 5,000, which amounts to 5 million barrels of oil. This is far less than what OPEC would need to hold to exert significant leverage in the market.

The second requirement, that OPEC establish a special agent to handle its trade, would be politically difficult. Members of OPEC have widely differing views about futures trading, ranging from mild support to strong opposition. It would be difficult to gain approval to engage formally in futures trading and to establish a trading agent.

An equally difficult issue is the financing of the agent's activities. As OPEC's primary reason for participating in futures trading would be to stabilize spot prices, the trading operations of the OPEC agent will likely result in a net loss. Thus, while OPEC members will gain benefits of a more stable spot market, they will have to pay for the offsetting futures transactions. The resulting questions are many. How should OPEC allocate the benefits of a more stable spot market among its members? Even more sensitive, how should the financing of the agent's activities be allocated among OPEC's members? Particularly in light of the disagreement among OPEC members on participation in the futures market, the question of financing will seriously impair the establishment of an OPEC futures trading agent.

The need for rapid decision-making acts as an informal barrier to OPEC's (in fact, any intergovernmental organization's) participation in futures trading. Futures contracts are bought and sold on the strength of market information that may only be relevant for a few minutes. A successful trader follows market trends and then makes his decision to buy or sell on the basis of information that is available at one particular moment. His decisions must be instantaneous. There is little time for him to consult with a governing body. If a futures trading agent were to succeed in achieving OPEC's goals, he would need to have clear guidelines on what he is to achieve and complete authority to act within these guidelines. Given the divergent views and goals of OPEC's thirteen members, it is highly unlikely that OPEC members would agree to give an agent the necessary instructions and authority.

The barriers to participation in futures trading by OPEC do not necessarily prevent individual members from trading with the aim of hedging against undesirable price movements or of securing a source of demand. To these ends, some OPEC members may sell crude oil and/or product futures.

In summary, futures markets have become the most visible part of the international petroleum market. They are now recognized as an efficient and reliable source of price information, but they have not changed the structure of the market, nor have they changed OPEC's power to control prices. For any level of OPEC output there is a market clearing price that will eventually prevail with or without futures (or even spot) markets. Spot markets make the market clearing price visible; futures markets accentuate this role. The development of futures markets has three important implications for OPEC:

- Direct or indirect administration of the market price is, as always, possible through adjustments in OPEC supply. But with the presence of futures markets, these adjustments have to be made very quickly. Futures markets work fast and make the entire market work faster;

- Because of the speed with which they process market reactions, futures markets may overreact and create excessive price fluctuations, but these fluctuations are very short term and need not worry the industry.
- The participation of OPEC as an organization in futures markets for the purposes of manipulating long-term price trends, speculation, or hedging is not feasible, but participation by individual members to hedge against a decline in crude and product prices is feasible.

Appendix Tables

Appendix Table 1
International Petroleum Markets
Official Prices, Spot Prices, and Netback Values of Various Crudes
Official Price, Spot Prices, and Netback Value of Arab Light-34 Average[a]
(US$/b FOB)

Year	Jan.	Feb.	March	April	May	June	July	Aug.	Sept.	Oct.	Nov.	Dec.
A. *Official Price*												
1978	12.70	12.70	12.70	12.70	12.70	12.70	12.70	12.70	12.70	12.70	12.70	12.70
1979	18.89	18.89	18.89	19.26	23.96	24.70	13.34	13.48	13.63	15.17	15.32	18.33
1980	29.20	30.70	30.70	30.00	32.00	32.00	26.90	27.30	27.30	28.65	28.90	28.90
1981	33.00	33.00	33.15	34.30	34.00	34.00	32.00	32.65	32.85	33.00	33.00	33.00
1982	33.60	33.60	33.50	33.40	33.30	33.00	34.00	33.85	33.55	33.50	33.40	33.40
1983	28.75	28.75	28.75	28.75	28.75	28.75	32.75	30.00	29.00	28.75	28.75	28.75
1984	28.75	28.75	28.75	28.75	28.75	28.75	28.75	28.75	28.75	28.75	28.75	28.75
1985	28.00	28.00	28.00	28.00	28.00	28.00	28.75	28.00	28.00	28.00	28.00	28.00
1986	—	—	—	—	—	—	—	—	—	—	—	—
1987	—	17.52	17.52	17.52	17.52	17.52	17.52	17.52	17.52	17.52	17.52	17.52
1988	17.52	17.52	17.52	17.52	17.52	17.52	17.52	17.52	17.52	17.52	17.52	17.52
B. *Spot Price*												
1978	12.66	12.66	12.66	12.68	12.70	12.73	12.77	12.79	12.80	12.85	13.20	14.50
1979	15.95	19.50	20.80	21.20	34.25	32.85	32.00	32.25	34.50	36.00	39.50	39.00
1980	38.00	36.00	35.75	35.00	35.60	36.00	33.35	32.30	32.25	36.80	39.75	39.35
1981	39.25	37.10	36.85	35.55	33.38	32.17	31.96	32.17	32.06	32.68	34.24	34.12
1982	34.00	30.40	28.60	30.88	33.35	32.65	31.70	31.20	33.05	33.40	31.75	30.10
1983	30.05	29.00	28.10	28.70	28.50	28.75	29.00	28.90	28.60	28.60	28.30	28.25

Year	Jan.	Feb.	March	April	May	June	July	Aug.	Sept.	Oct.	Nov.	Dec.
1984	28.60	28.56	28.53	28.39	28.43	28.11	27.53	27.64	27.80	27.89	27.94	27.59
1985	27.91	27.73	27.73	27.65	26.92	26.75	27.06	27.44	27.61	27.79	27.90	27.90
1986	26.15	16.30	12.90	12.00	12.80	—	—	—	—	—	—	—
1987	—	—	17.30	17.35	17.30	17.50	17.75	17.75	17.45	17.40	17.15	16.50
1988	15.80	15.60	13.75	15.05	15.00	14.00	13.35	13.25	11.80	10.60	10.85	12.75
1989	14.70	15.00	16.40	17.95	16.90	16.05	15.90	15.30	16.10	17.00	17.00	17.80

C. *Netback Value*

Year	Jan.	Feb.	March	April	May	June	July	Aug.	Sept.	Oct.	Nov.	Dec.
1978	12.63	12.46	12.64	12.70	12.81	12.72	12.66	13.06	13.01	13.20	15.06	14.24
1979	16.33	22.21	22.13	23.61	27.82	31.76	30.61	29.89	30.23	31.74	34.65	35.68
1980	33.83	31.07	30.32	31.44	32.08	30.90	30.32	28.72	28.92	32.90	36.10	34.55
1981	34.92	35.09	34.33	33.52	31.53	29.83	30.86	30.78	31.33	31.96	32.62	32.10
1982	31.39	29.85	27.96	29.13	31.25	31.53	30.16	30.34	31.33	31.78	30.74	29.51
1983	28.96	26.89	26.15	27.85	27.63	27.74	27.99	28.41	28.27	27.97	27.71	26.54
1984	27.55	27.47	27.47	27.95	27.99	27.05	26.15	25.95	26.59	26.73	26.20	25.72
1985	25.78	26.52	26.33	26.11	24.51	24.18	24.34	24.62	25.06	25.45	25.93	24.78
1986	21.30	18.80	17.02	14.23	13.65	11.02	8.87	11.45	12.49	11.94	12.35	13.09
1987	17.70	15.37	16.46	17.19	17.38	17.25	17.55	16.57	16.31	17.30	16.12	15.06
1988	14.39	13.81	13.36	15.32	14.91	14.19	13.35	13.30	12.35	11.77	12.89	13.68
1989	14.91	14.80	16.34	19.06	17.56	15.94	16.07	15.78	16.76	17.71	17.61	20.00

a. Prices after 1985 are those of Arab Light-34 Average.

Source: Petroleum Intelligence Weekly, various issues. New York.

Appendix Table 2
International Petroleum Markets
Official Prices, Spot Prices, and Netback Value of Various Crudes
Official Price, Spot Price, and Netback Value of Nigerian Light 37/44[a]
(US$/b FOB)

Year	Jan.	Feb.	March	Apr.	May	June	July	Aug.	Sept.	Oct.	Nov.	Dec.
A. Official Price												
1978	14.20	14.20	14.20	13.95	13.95	13.95	13.90	13.90	13.90	13.95	13.95	13.95
1979	14.20	14.20	14.20	13.95	13.95	13.95	13.90	13.90	13.90	13.95	13.95	13.95
1980	33.10	35.45	35.45	35.65	37.25	37.25	38.15	38.15	36.90	36.90	36.90	36.90
1981	40.30	40.30	40.30	40.30	40.30	40.30	39.90	39.90	38.70	38.25	37.07	37.00
1982	36.75	35.85	34.65	34.05	34.05	34.90	34.90	34.70	34.50	34.25	34.25	34.10
1983	34.00	32.10	30.80	30.25	30.20	30.20	30.20	30.20	30.20	30.20	30.20	30.20
1984	30.20	30.20	30.20	30.20	30.20	30.20	30.20	30.20	30.20	29.35	29.35	29.35
1985	28.90	29.00	29.00	29.00	29.00	29.00	29.00	29.00	29.00	29.00	29.00	29.00
1986	—	—	—	—	—	—	—	—	—	—	—	—
1987	—	18.92	18.92	18.92	18.92	18.92	18.92	18.92	18.92	18.92	18.92	18.92
1988	18.92	18.92	18.92	18.92	18.92	18.92	18.92	18.92	18.92	18.92	18.92	18.92
B. Spot Price												
1978	14.05	14.00	13.95	13.83	13.90	13.95	13.89	13.96	14.09	14.35	14.90	16.25
1979	14.05	14.00	13.95	13.83	13.90	13.95	13.89	13.96	14.09	14.35	14.90	16.25
1980	40.00	38.50	38.25	38.15	38.50	38.00	37.40	33.60	33.40	37.90	40.85	40.15
1981	40.30	38.70	38.35	37.19	35.19	33.25	35.06	35.80	35.91	36.54	37.12	36.70
1982	35.85	31.62	29.30	33.12	35.18	34.60	33.70	32.85	34.25	35.00	33.80	31.75
1983	30.85	29.10	28.20	29.75	29.60	30.20	30.80	31.10	30.35	29.85	29.20	28.95
1984	29.45	29.77	29.99	30.05	29.86	28.94	27.87	28.09	28.45	28.26	27.74	27.24

Year	Jan.	Feb.	March	Apr.	May	June	July	Aug.	Sept.	Oct.	Nov.	Dec.
1985	27.16	28.08	28.15	28.15	26.79	26.59	27.04	27.54	27.94	28.80	30.10	26.85
1986	22.90	18.00	13.90	12.70	14.40	11.90	9.55	13.75	14.20	13.80	14.60	15.90
1987	18.45	17.55	18.05	18.35	18.80	18.95	19.95	19.05	18.50	19.00	18.10	17.15
1988	16.95	15.90	14.85	16.75	16.50	15.65	15.10	15.10	13.40	12.55	13.15	15.45
1989	17.35	17.15	19.05	20.55	18.95	17.90	17.95	16.90	17.95	19.20	19.15	20.25

C. Netback Value

Year	Jan.	Feb.	March	Apr.	May	June	July	Aug.	Sept.	Oct.	Nov.	Dec.
1978	13.71	13.50	13.88	14.13	14.29	14.06	14.14	14.82	14.82	15.42	18.23	16.79
1979	13.71	13.50	13.88	14.13	14.29	14.06	14.14	14.82	14.82	15.42	18.23	16.79
1980	38.32	35.80	34.82	32.27	35.98	34.83	34.10	31.58	31.58	34.25	37.18	34.97
1981	37.10	37.57	37.03	36.12	34.26	32.92	34.15	34.41	34.86	35.52	36.24	35.72
1982	35.00	32.96	30.53	31.83	34.47	34.62	32.95	33.29	34.57	35.03	33.69	32.06
1983	31.28	28.64	27.42	29.51	29.67	29.84	30.07	30.36	30.04	29.42	29.28	28.26
1984	29.40	29.37	29.08	29.10	28.83	27.91	27.91	27.07	27.67	27.50	26.95	26.30
1985	26.40	27.22	27.40	27.67	26.57	26.58	26.25	26.37	27.40	28.15	28.77	26.92
1986	23.75	20.79	18.78	16.34	15.94	12.53	10.05	12.93	14.11	13.42	13.78	14.60
1987	19.22	17.16	17.68	18.15	18.57	18.52	19.26	18.51	17.96	18.99	18.17	17.25
1988	16.49	15.60	15.12	17.20	16.94	16.07	15.55	15.49	14.37	13.87	15.35	16.46
1989	17.45	16.83	18.25	21.50	19.72	17.82	17.97	17.56	19.06	20.09	19.84	22.61

a. Prices after 1985 are those of Nigerian Light 37.

Source: Petroleum Intelligence Weekly, various issues. New York.

Appendix Table 3

Number of Petroleum Contracts Traded on the New York Mercantile Exchange (NYMEX)

Year	Jan.	Feb.	March	April	May	June	July	Aug.	Sept.	Oct.	Nov.	Dec.
A. Heating oil												
1978	—	—	—	—	—	—	—	—	—	—	37	79
1979	365	515	182	369	502	1,337	2,156	2,205	2,857	5,895	9,371	8,010
1980	8,512	8,427	5,146	5,898	3,421	5,923	6,074	11,564	27,430	40,525	53,098	63,366
1981	67,368	58,514	55,299	65,350	58,933	76,580	86,394	100,102	99,790	121,455	78,973	126,749
1982	165,029	148,794	176,373	146,821	98,440	135,181	107,102	118,496	120,830	167,439	177,832	183,139
1983	153,864	112,649	137,237	121,300	163,923	149,138	138,709	140,671	187,283	169,271	200,400	193,877
1984	254,788	209,802	141,326	144,041	161,689	141,182	120,668	153,913	137,011	281,183	182,005	163,938
1985	286,264	149,403	162,503	137,064	122,699	133,339	148,117	157,552	202,785	246,550	216,429	242,323
1986	274,057	221,156	214,501	207,748	223,943	247,552	309,662	282,636	285,246	387,454	271,497	349,992
1987	333,675	405,107	399,663	367,102	303,675	286,742	232,880	247,291	294,114	334,327	297,022	519,643
1988	506,182	377,379	403,189	267,233	286,365	380,550	431,281	363,276	441,939	578,698	475,675	423,356
1989	534,041	422,600	430,447	372,640	334,973	445,822	572,388	402,420	473,402	554,733	579,693	820,748
1990	754,345	415,420	462,479	451,708	316,989	463,265	518,993					
B. Gasoline (leaded regular)												
1981	—	—	—	—	—	—	—	—	—	2,363	1,384	3,553
1982	4,206	3,750	4,292	5,243	13,153	15,040	7,814	6,395	7,361	9,764	9,109	17,955
1983	22,960	20,422	35,333	35,391	35,723	31,429	24,512	26,405	34,536	35,745	47,380	57,007
1984	77,515	70,141	60,822	68,837	81,870	76,003	59,185	50,082	26,862	28,978	23,394	29,941
1985	49,776	49,554	62,106	56,492	67,001	58,551	54,770	58,571	49,709	66,662	40,949	53,063
1986	81,277	75,816	84,519	128,683	137,796	113,336	103,311	77,845	23,345	1,806	Terminated on 11/31	
1987	77,652	96,399	129,475	158,759	194,227	209,894	190,473	175,732	176,806	158,409	142,776	180,486

Year	Jan.	Feb.	March	April	May	June	July	Aug.	Sept.	Oct.	Nov.	Dec.
C. Gasoline (unleaded)												
1984	—	—	—	—	—	—	—	—	—	—	—	2,736
1985	9,042	4,045	7,848	10,093	10,853	12,219	19,532	16,403	10,604	15,808	8,427	7,737
1986	13,478	11,914	9,459	7,352	14,033	10,288	12,878	17,396	55,329	105,884	74,711	107,630
1987	135,208	139,883	211,590	214,982	178,735	175,583	181,661	154,665	155,352	166,365	152,376	190,014
1988	196,616	191,231	245,019	217,139	257,507	330,009	401,186	254,010	294,542	355,982	302,438	240,366
1989	354,161	252,669	373,930	510,069	407,445	443,205	356,939	310,346	412,753	375,489	328,271	352,168
1990	540,633	394,437	461,438	481,665	527,637	472,377	456,342					
D. Crude oil (WTI)												
1983	—	—	3,362	16,924	16,546	15,902	18,566	17,311	26,536	46,092	67,191	97,733
1984	108,743	130,712	121,476	106,227	136,420	134,468	154,938	200,416	111,200	243,328	174,746	217,668
1985	385,272	262,293	298,547	272,575	290,073	342,216	329,768	269,735	339,771	365,945	337,892	386,780
1986	520,070	490,948	559,960	691,382	677,042	612,651	860,326	701,636	666,732	986,419	609,389	941,779
1987	749,053	843,866	912,566	1,033,076	1,171,444	1,040,220	925,108	1,023,603	1,235,074	1,444,684	1,156,224	1,451,540
1988	1,625,656	1,335,551	1,809,360	1,351,662	1,205,266	1,506,699	1,753,639	1,215,764	1,955,869	2,090,392	1,603,430	1,449,660
1989	1,919,061	1,524,189	2,052,721	2,070,470	1,910,713	2,081,648	1,662,646	1,343,330	1,541,011	1,521,283	1,425,246	1,482,547
1990	2,163,851	1,789,688	1,794,496	1,812,959	1,944,876	1,839,015	2,046,268					

Notes

1. Petroleum Argus keeps detailed records of spot transactions in the Brent market as a basis for their daily and weekly reports. They distinguish between "dated" and "fifteen-day" contracts. Their records begin in late July 1983 and continue to the present. For detailed discussion, see Mabro, et al., *The Market for North Sea Crude Oil*, Oxford University Press, London, 1986.
2. Mabro, et al., *The Market for North Sea Crude Oil*, p. 198.
3. Indonesia's incentive to adhere to the official price was not only to follow OPEC agreements but also to preserve its revenue from the sale of liquefied natural gas (LNG), the price of which is linked to the official price of Indonesian crudes.
4. *Petroleum Intelligence Weekly*, October 8, 1979.
5. The Saudi Arabian production quota was adjusted to 4.35 million b/d in 1984.
6. J. Roeber, "The Rotterdam Oil Market," *Petroleum Economist*, April 1979.
7. See European Commission's press release in *Petroleum Intelligence Weekly*, September 14, 1979.
8. A forward contract is an agreement for the sale (or purchase) of a commodity at a specified time in the future at a certain price.
9. *Energy in the News*, third quarter 1988.
10. Based on examples worked out by Leiffer and Harwitt (1988), Colburn (1988), and Kaplan and Beutel (1988).
11. Economists define precautionary stock as a counterpart to speculative stock. Normally, speculative stocks are built when the stockpiler anticipates a price increase, that is, when the expected mean of the price is increasing. On the other hand, precautionary stocks are built if uncertainty about the price, that is, the variance of the price, is large. In oil market analysis, the term *speculative stock* is used in the same context as in economics. However, the term *precautionary stock* is used in a much more limited sense than in economics. It refers to the additional inventory held to cope with normal interruptions in the operation of the petroleum industry.

12. This is an inquiry about the hypothesis that "futures contracts encompass some information about the relevant future events and thereby reflect the future trends of the spot market price."
13. This point will be elaborated later when the basic characteristics of futures prices are discussed.
14. Even at $10.00–12.00/b, Saudi Arabia could not be said to be comfortable. See the Economist Intelligence Unit's *Middle East Quarterly Energy Review* No. 3, 1985; see also "OPEC's Finances," *Petroleum Intelligence Weekly*, January 13, 1985, and "Price War Vulnerability: Who Feels First Pinch," *Petroleum Intelligence Weekly*, February 10, 1985.

Glossary of Terms

Actuals: The physical or cash commodity.

Arbitrage: The simultaneous purchase and sale of different contracts to profit from an expected change in the price differentials between them. The contracts can be for different commodities, for the same commodity in different locations, or for the same commodity at the same location but for different months.

Backwardation: When the price of a good for later delivery stands below the price of the good for earlier delivery. That is, nearby futures trade at a premium to the more distant futures.

Basis: Describes a price based on another price. In futures trading, basis is used to show:
1. the difference between the prices of two commodities;
2. the difference between the prices of the same commodity in different locations; or
3. the difference between the prices of the same commodity at the same location but for different delivery months.

Bear: A person who sells with the expectation of a price fall.

Bid: An offer to buy at a stated price.

Broker: A person paid a fee or commission for acting as an agent in making contracts or sales.

Brokerage: A fee charged by a broker for execution of a transaction.

Bull: A person who buys with the expectation of a price rise.

Bunker C: Residual fuel oil.

Buying hedge: Buying futures contracts equal to the amount of the cash commodity that is eventually needed.

Cash and carry: The simultaneous purchase of a commodity for cash delivery and sale of the same delivery at a later date.

Cash market: The actual or physical market (spot market).

Carrying charge: The cost to store and ensure the delivery of a physical commodity.

CFTC: Commodity Futures Trading Commission in the United States.

Chicago Board of Trade (CBT): The world's largest futures exchange, founded in 1848 in Chicago.

Chicago Mercantile Exchange (CME): The world's second largest futures exchange, founded in 1919 in Chicago.

Clearinghouse: A nonprofit association that helps its members balance their accounts with one another.

Contango: To gain control of the market to sell at inflated prices.

Crack spread: Simultaneous sale and purchase of crude and products contracts.

Day order: An order that only applies for one trading day.

Day trading: A purchase and sale of the same futures during the trading hours of a single day.

Deep in (out of) the money: A situation in which the strike price of an option is substantially more (less) favorable than the current price of the underlying commodity.

Delivery notice: Notice of a clearing member's intention to deliver a stated quantity of a commodity in settlement of a futures contract.

Delta: Measure of probability that an option will have certain value at expiration date.

Deposit: The initial outlay required by a broker to open a futures position.

Differentials: Price differences between qualities and locations of delivery.

Discretionary account: An account for which buying and selling orders are decided by the broker without the prior consent of the client.

First notice day: The first day on which a notice of intention to deliver the actual commodity against a futures contract can be made.

Floor broker: A member who executes orders for the accounts of other members on the trading floor.

Forward contract: An agreement to make and take the delivery of a commodity in the future. A forward contract is normally tailored to the particular needs of the contracting parties.

Futures contract: A commitment to make or accept delivery of a specified (standardized) quantity and quality of a commodity during a specific month in the future at a price agreed at the time the commitment was made.

Good till canceled (GTC): An open order that remains in force until the client explicitly cancels the order, or until the futures contract expires.

Hedge: To use the futures market to reduce the price risks associated with buying and selling the actual commodity.

IPE: International Petroleum Exchange formed in 1981 in London for trading petroleum futures contracts.

Inverted market: When the nearby futures trade at a premium to the more distant futures.

Last trading day: The last day for trading a particular delivery.

Limit: The maximum fluctuation that is allowed on certain markets in one trading session.

Limit order: An order to buy or sell at a specified price.

Liquidation: The closing out of a previous position by taking an opposite position in the same contract.

Long: Describes the market position of someone who has purchased something. In futures trading, it refers to the purchase of a futures contract without an offsetting sale.

Long liquidation: The closing of long positions.

Lot: The minimum contract size for a particular commodity.

Margin: A deposit that a client makes with his broker to secure the performance of the futures contract.

Margin call: A broker's request to a client for additional funds to keep his original deposit intact a certain percentage of the contract value.

Market order: An order to buy or sell at the best obtainable price.

NYMEX: Founded in 1872, the New York Mercantile Exchange is currently the world's largest petroleum futures market.

Netback: (as in netback pricing) The net value of products manufactured from the underlying crude.

Open interest: The number of contracts for futures delivery outstanding at any time, i.e., the number of contracts that have not been canceled by an offsetting trade.

Pit: The area on an exchange floor where futures trading of a commodity takes place.

Bibliography

R. Anderson, and M. Sundaresan. July 1983. "Futures Markets and Monopoly." Working Paper CSFM-63. New York: Center for the Study of Futures Markets, Columbia University.

Angell, G. 1979. *Winning in the Commodities Market*. New York: Doubleday.

Architzel, P. M., and J. P. Connolly. 1981. "Delivery on Futures Contracts as a Legal Requirement." *Business Lawyer*, Vol. 36 (April 1981): pp. 935–952.

Bacon, R. 1984. "A Study of the Relationship between Spot Product Prices and Spot Crude Prices." Oxford, England: Oxford Institute for Energy Studies.

Baesel, J., and D. Grant. 1982. "Equilibrium in a Futures Market." *Southern Economic Journal*, Vol. 49 (1982): pp. 320–329.

Bodie, Z., and V. Rosansky. October 1979. "Risk and Return in Commodity Futures." Working Paper 1. New York: Center for the Study of Futures Markets, Columbia University.

Breeden, D. T. April 1983. "Futures Markets and Commodity Options: Hedging and Optimality in Incomplete Markets." Working Paper CSFM-52. New York: Center for the Study of Futures Markets, Columbia University.

Brennan, M. J. 1985. "The Supply of Storage." *American Economic Review*, Vol. 48 (1985): pp. 50–72.

Burns, J. M. 1979. *A Treatise on Markets: Spot, Futures, and Options*. Washington, D.C.: American Enterprise Institute.

Chassard, C. 1987. *Option Trading and Oil Futures Markets*. Oxford, England: Oxford Institute for Energy Studies.

Chevron Corporation. 1985. *Crude and Product Market Perspective*, December 17, 1985.

Colburn, J. 1988. "Hedging with Heating Oil Options." *Energy in the News*, Third Quarter 1988.

Dow Jones and Company, Inc. 1981. *The ABC's of Option Trading*. Chicopee.

El-Serafy, S. 1982. "Absorptive Capacity, the Demand for Revenue, and the Supply of Petroleum." *Journal of Energy and Development* (Vol. 6): pp. 16-29.

Energy Information Administration. Various issues. *Monthly Energy Review*. Washington, D.C.

Exxon Corporation. 1981. "World Oil Inventories." *Exxon Background Series*, August 1981.

————. 1980. "Middle East Oil." *Exxon Background Series*, September 1980.

Farmer, R. D. 1983. "Determinants of Distillate Inventory Levels: An Economic Analysis of Declining Stocks in 1982." Washington, D.C.: Energy Information Administration, U.S. Department of Energy. February 1983.

Farnon, P. 1981. "The Rotterdam Oil Market." *Vision* (April 1981): Vol. 35, pp. 12–17.

Fesharaki, F. 1984. "The Singapore Story: A Refining Center in a Transitory Oil Market." Honolulu: Resource Systems Institute, East-West Center (April 1984).

————. 1985. "Oil Trading in the Asia-Pacific Basin: The Role of Singapore as an Oil Trading Center." Keynote Address to the First International Conference on Oil Trading Activities and Opportunities in the Asia-Pacific Basin, September 1985.

Fesharaki, F., and D. D. Isaak. 1983. *OPEC, the Gulf and the World Petroleum Market*. Boulder, Colo.: Westview Press.

————. 1984. "OPEC and Asia: Factors Affecting the Emerging Product Trade." Paper presented at the Seventh Asia-Pacific Energy Studies Consultative Group, September 5–7, 1984.

————. 1984. *OPEC and the World Refining Crisis*. Special Report No. 168. London: The Economist Intelligence Unit. April 1984.

Frankel, P. 1962. *Oil: The Facts of Life*. London: Charles Birchall and Sons, Ltd.

Friedman, D. G. W. Harrison, and J. W. Salmon. 1982. "The International Role of Futures Markets: Some Experimental Evidence." Working Paper CSFM-50. New York: Center for the Study of Futures Markets, Columbia University. December 1982.

Gold, G. 1973. *Modern Commodity Futures Trading*. New York: Commodity Research Bureau, Inc.

Goss, B. A., and B. S. Yamey. 1976. *The Economics of Futures Trading: Selected Readings*. New York: John Wiley and Sons.

Greaves, W. 1985. "The Use of Futures to Determine Prices in Sales Contracts." Paper presented at conference entitled "Practical Applications of Futures Trading for the Oil Industry," May 9, 1985.

Haar, L. 1984. "The Role and Importance of Crude and Product Futures Markets." Paper presented at the meetings of the International Association of Energy Economics, New Delhi, January 1984.

Hieronymus, T. A. 1971. *Economics of Futures Trading*. New York: Commodity Research Bureau, Inc.

Houthakker, H. S. 1957. "Can Speculators Forecast Prices?" *Review of Economics and Statistics*, Vol. 39, pp. 143–157.

———. 1982. "The Extension of Futures Trading to the Financial Sector." *Journal of Banking and Finance*, Vol. 6, pp. 37–47.

Jain, A. K. 1980. "Commodity Futures Markets and the Law of the One Price." Ann Arbor: University of Michigan.

Johnson, L. L. "The Theory of Hedging and Speculation in Commodity Futures." *Review of Economic Studies*, Vol. 27, No. 3, pp. 139–151.

Kamara, A. 1982. "Issues in Futures Markets: A Survey." Working Paper CSFM-30. New York: Center for the Study of Futures Markets, Columbia University Business School. March 1982.

Kaplan, D. E., and P. C. Beutel. 1988. "A Winter Hedge Strategy for a Heating Oil Distributor." *Energy in the News*, Third Quarter 1988. New York.

Kay, J. B. 1988. "Option Trading Strategies." *Energy in the News*, Third Quarter 1988. New York.

Keng, L. T. 1985. *A Feasibility Study of Developing Oil Futures Exchange in Singapore*. Thesis submitted to National University of Singapore, Singapore, March 1985.

Krapels, E. N. 1983. "Growing Influence of Oil Stocks." *Petroleum Economist*, June 1983, pp. 211–214.

Leiffer, R., and J. Harwitt. 1988. "The Practical Application of Heating Oil Options." *Energy in the News*, Third Quarter, 1988.

Loosigian, A. M. 1980. *Interest Rate Futures*. Homewood, Ill.: Dow Jones-Irwin.

Lower, R. C. 1979. "The Regulation of Commodity Options." *Duke Law Journal*, Vol. 1978, No. 5.

Mabro, R. 1979. "OPEC, Oil Nationalism, and the U.S. Elephant." *Petroleum Intelligence Weekly*, April 30, 1979.

———. 1982. "Can OPEC Hold the Price Line?" *Middle East Economic Survey*, Special Supplement, March 8, 1982.

————. 1982. "The Changing Nature of the Oil Market and OPEC Policies." *Middle East Economic Survey*, September 20, 1982.

Mabro, R., et al. 1986. *The Market for North Sea Crude Oil*. London: Oxford University Press.

National Petroleum Council. 1983. *Petroleum Inventories and Storage Capacity*. Washington, D.C.: National Petroleum Council. November 1983.

Neftei, S., and A. J. Policano. 1983. "Can Chartists Outperform the Market?" Working Paper Series CSFM-53. New York: Center for the Study of Futures Markets, Columbia University. April 1983.

New York Mercantile Exchange. 1984. "The Crack Spread News." *A Special Energy Report*. New York. January 1984.

Newberry, D. M. G., and J. E. Stiglitz. 1981. *The Theory of Commodity Price Stabilization*. Oxford: Clarendon Press.

Nichols, A. L., and R. L. Zeckhauser. 1977. "Stockpiling Strategies and Cartel Prices." *Bell Journal of Economics*, Volume 9, pp. 39–45.

Niering, F. E. 1983. "Can New Markets Help Price Stability?" *Petroleum Economist*, June 1983, pp. 223–227.

————. 1984. "The Spot Market." *Petroleum Economist*, January 1984.

————. Various years. *Annual Statistical Bulletin*. Organization of the Petroleum Exporting Countries.

Para, A. A. 1982. "OPEC Move May Lead to Structured Market." *Petroleum Intelligence Weekly*, April 12, 1982.

Peck, A. E., ed. 1977. *Selected Writings on Futures Markets*. Chicago: Board of Trade of the City of Chicago.

Powers, M. J. 1970. "Does Futures Trading Reduce Price Fluctuations in the Cash Market?" *American Economic Review*, 1970, pp. 460–464.

Prast, W. G., and H. L. Lax. 1983. *Oil Future Markets*. Lexington: Lexington Books.

Preston, M. H., and B. S. Yamey. 1960. "Inter-Temporal Price Relationships with Forward Markets: A Method of Analysis." *Economica*, Vol. 37, pp. 335–337.

Razavi, H. 1982. "Optimal Rate of Oil Production for OPEC Member Countries." *Resources and Energy*, 1982, pp. 291–305.

————. 1983. "An Analysis of Iran's Oil Production Policy." *Applied Economics*, April 1983.

————. 1983. "Effect of Uncertainty on Oil Extraction Decisions." *Journal of Economic Dynamics and Control*, September 1983.

————. 1984. "An Economic Model of OPEC Coalition." *Southern Economic Journal*, October 1984.

———. 1984. *Oil Futures Trading: The Impact on the Structure of the Petroleum Industry*. London: Financial Times Business Information.

———. 1985. "Oil Production and Economic Development in Mexico." *The Energy Journal*, April 1985.

Razavi, H., and F. Fesharaki. 1984. "Interactions between Crude and Refined Oil Markets." *Energy Policy*, June 1984.

Razavi, H., and M. V. Samii. 1982. "Conditions for the Short-Term and Long-Term Stability of OPEC." *OPEC Review*, Vol. 6 (Winter 1982).

Roeber, J. 1979. "The Rotterdam Oil Market." *Petroleum Economist*, April 1979.

Rowan, H. S., and J. B. Weyant. 1982. "Reducing the Economic Impacts of Oil Supply Interruptions: An International Perspective." *The Energy Journal*, 1982.

Samuelson, P. A. 1976. "Is Real-World Price a Tale Told by the Idiot of Chance?" *Review of Economics and Statistics*, Vol. 58 (1976): pp. 120–123.

Shell Briefing Service. 1984. "Trading Oil." London: Royal Dutch/Shell Group.

———. 1984. "Changes in the Oil Supply System." London: Royal Dutch/Shell Group.

Stein, J. L. 1961. "The Simultaneous Determination of Spot and Futures Prices." *American Economic Review* (December 1961).

Stevenson, R. A., and R. M. Bear. 1970. "Commodity Futures: Trends or Random Walks?" *Journal of Finance* (March 1970): pp. 65–81.

Tahmassebi, H. February 1984. "Crude Oil and Product Differentials." Ashland Oil Company.

Teisberg, T. J. 1981. "A Dynamic Programming Model of the US Strategic Petroleum Reserve." *The Bell Journal of Economics* (Autumn 1981).

Thomas, M. 1984. "The ABCs of Measuring Oil Market Price Trends." *Petroleum Intelligence Week*.

Tomek, W. G., and R. W. Gray. 1970. "Temporal Relationships among Prices on Commodity Futures Markets: Their Allocative and Stabilizing Roles." *American Journal of Agricultural Economics*, Vol. 52 (August 1970).

Treat, J. E. 1984. "Energy Futures and World Oil Markets." Paper presented at the meeting of the International Association of Energy Economists, New Delhi, January 1984.

———. 1984. *Energy Futures*. Tulsa, Oklahoma: PennWell Publishing Company.

U.S. General Accounting Office. 1980. *The United States Exerts Limited Influence on the International Crude Oil Spot Market.* Report of the Congress of the United States, August 21, 1980.

Verleger, P. 1982. *Oil Markets in Turmoil: An Economic Analysis.* Cambridge, Mass.: Ballinger Publishing Co.

William, J. C. 1980. *The Economic Function of Futures Markets.* Unpublished Ph.D. dissertation, Yale University, December 1980.

Working, H. 1953. "Futures Trading and Hedging." *American Economic Review*, 1953, pp. 314–343.

Wright, B. D., and J. C. Williams. 1982. "The Economic Role of Commodity Storage." *The Economic Journal*, September 1982.

———. 1982. "The Roles of Public and Private Storage in Managing Oil Import Disruptions." *The Bell Journal of Economics*, 1982, pp. 341–353.

Zimmerman, J. 1980. "The Rotterdam Market: Confusion and Crisis in the Petroleum Industry." Thesis submitted to Princeton University, Princeton, New Jersey, April 11, 1980.

Index

ABOUT THE AUTHORS

Hossein Razavi is Principal Energy Economist at the World Bank. He has published extensively in the field of energy. His recent contributions have appeared in the *Energy Journal, Energy Policy, Energy Economics, Applied Energy, Annual Review of Energy, Resources and Energy,* and several books by the Economist Intelligence Unit and Financial Times Business Information. He holds a Ph.D. in economics and a master's of science in engineering.

Fereidun Fesharaki is the Energy Program Leader at the Resource Systems Institute, East-West Center, in Honolulu. He is the author or co-author of 16 books and monographs and numerous articles in the field of energy. He holds a Ph.D. in economics.